Copyrig

All rights reserved

The characters and events portrayed in this book are fictitious. Any similarity to real persons, living or dead, is coincidental and not intended by the author.

No part of this book may be reproduced, or stored in a retrieval system, or transmitted in any form or by any means, electronic, mechanical, photocopying, recording, or otherwise, without express written permission of the publisher.

Cover design by: R. R. Skrycki

ISBN: 9798553807450
Printed in the United States of America
Non-fiction
1. Autobiography-memoirs
2. Biography-people with disabilities

STOLEN CAKE

Embracing the Alzheimer's-Caregiver Role

R. R. Skrycki

PROLOGUE

Like ghosts locked in a closet, the remnants of a life parade behind the glass doors of a china cabinet, free from dust, yet sadly, also free from the memories that once held them dear. The oldest whispers from the past include the floral china gravy dish that her parents received as a wedding gift in 1907 and the small pewter boat sailing on a sea of blue glass, which she bought with her babysitting money as a wedding gift to her sister in 1931. The top shelf parades the delicate flower-etched crystal stemware she received as a wedding gift when she married in 1942. A few shelves down sits the slightly tarnished silver ice decanter that once shined to serve an array of family and friends on the Christmas Eves she entertained in the home they lovingly built in 1963. On the same shelf sits the glass cake dish passed down from her mother, which held countless homemade birthday cakes topped with buttermilk icing (a family recipe). And finally, the bottom shelf now holds the golf scene brackets that adorned the corners of her husband's casket when he was laid to rest in 2001. These small mementos weave together the tattered fabric of what was once a richly vibrant life. The memory and the date was written on the bottom of each object, as if the writer knew those memories would soon fail her, so she preserved them for loved ones. For her, slices of those sweet memories are missing. A criminal named Alzheimer's disease is stealing them away.

PART 1

THE PROMISE

1

It all began on a typical brisk November morning. On that morning of my birthday in 2001 I was expecting to receive a phone call from my parents wishing me a happy birthday. This annual routine included a re-telling of my birth at 7:00 in the morning and what a glorious day that was. But there was nothing usual about this day. Beginning today, that routine would change forever.

When my mother, Ruth, finally called me about 11:00 a.m., it took several shocking seconds to absorb what she was saying. I was *not* expecting to hear that my dad, Harold, was unresponsive and the ambulance was taking him to the hospital. I hurriedly left work to fetch my mother so we could join up with my dad at the hospital. Other family members arrived, and it wasn't long before the doctor herded our family into a small room to deliver the devastating diagnosis of a massive stroke. I felt a sense of urgency to go in to visit him alone, believing this could be our last visit together. He was looking at me, but was unable to speak. My pillar, my decision-maker, now lay inert on a hospital bed as others are making decisions for him. Unexplainably, I felt a calm come over me as I reached for his hand, on the side that wasn't paralyzed, and held it in mine. I prayed to ask Jesus to come into our hearts. Looking directly into my eyes, he squeezed my hand back, and I believe he was telling me with nonverbal cues that he understood. That evening of my birthday, my father's spirit was reborn, and later on that same night, his spirit left this earth and was born into heaven. Before he left us, I assured him there was no cause for worry about Mom; I promised to take care of her. There was no way I could know at that time of a different disease that had already begun to ravage her brain.

The grieving process itself gives rise to confusion. Suddenly, for my mother, the man she was married to for fifty-nine years is no longer there. Life becomes a whole new ballgame. A new routine began for me as well with Sunday morning breakfasts and Wednesday evening dinners, as well as regular visits to the library with Mom. As the days wore on, it seemed as if her confusion grew more intense rather than less. Grief has no time limit, but if her confusion was caused by grief, wouldn't the confusion memory lapses begin to subside? Six months later, my sisters, Leslie and Laurie, and I, scheduled an appointment for her with a neuropsychologist. The extensive testing confirmed the diagnosis—Alzheimer's disease, or AD. After our initial horror, a new grief took hold of her with the cruelty of knowing what she would soon face, and the pall of a shadow settled over our lives. We took her home, and the tears began to flow all around like melting glaciers sliding down the mountainside from where they once had a sure foothold in time.

Our lives, as we knew them, were going to change once again. I became a regular e-mail subscriber to the *Alzheimer's Association*. Mom was prescribed a memory medication. The disease did not sneak up and kidnap her thoughts right away, but rather it would snatch a memory here or a function there when she least expected it. She nobly fought the thief with every weapon she had. Organization became a very effective implement. We arranged her medications into a pill box and began a calendar, outlining her daily functions. We crossed out the days gone by, and she came to rely on her calendar as a daily tool to function. The neuropsychologist said that her higher level of intelligence would allow her to hide the memory loss, and this did indeed become her favorite weapon of choice. She could even fool her doctors, fabricating the answers to their questions by saying whatever she felt they were expecting to hear. I would have to take the doctors aside and tell them what was fact and what was fiction, but I suppose it gave her a sense that she was still in control of her answers. For several years, no one would even know she had the dreaded disease, unless we gave away the secret.

2

A number of years ago, my parents appointed me as power of attorney over their financial affairs. This was due largely to my paralegal degree, and having some experience working in law offices. My parents lived a legacy of loving all three daughters and treating us equally and fairly all our lives. I believed a living trust would be the best way to protect Mom's assets and her wishes, especially if anything were to happen to me while she still needed care. AD is a very expensive disease.

We met with an attorney who prepared her will and trust, spelling out her wishes for equal distribution upon her demise. It was also necessary to prepare an updated power of attorney because according to the privacy laws, doctors cannot give you any information about their patient without one. She also signed a medical power of attorney, so the medical community would have a clear direction for her medical wishes when she was no longer able to speak for herself. These documents were prepared while she was still of sound mind, so there would be no confusion as to her wishes. It is easy for families to be ripped apart during the illness or death of a parent, and I didn't want that to happen to us. Money can drive a wedge between even the most loving of families. It was very important to me through this process that my sisters were to be kept informed, and I solicited and welcomed their input on all major decisions. I provided them with an annual accounting of expenditures to prevent misunderstandings. This is all part of the caregiving process.

3

Statistics show that the population is aging. Research suggests that for most of human existence, the life span has been thirty years or less. Over the last two hundred years, things have dramatically changed. Due to advanced medical technologies, improvement in nutrition, sanitation, and medical care, today the average life span in a large part of the world is over eighty years of age. Most shockingly, however, is that conservative statistics also reveal that at least 40 percent of people over the age of eighty can expect to experience some form of dementia.

More and more people are aging, yet a large percentage of these will need someone to care for them, and in fact, a good number of caregivers will be needed for each individual who suffers from the devastating illness of Alzheimer's disease or some other form of dementia. You can expect the care will require a team effort. It could happen to a parent, an aunt or uncle, a spouse, a sibling, a cousin, or a friend. This global crisis calls many who are unprepared to become a caregiver at some point in their life, or in the very least, they will know a caregiver who could use some help. In fact, dementia and AD are affecting more and more people *under* the age of eighty, as in the "early onset" form of the disease that can strike people in their forties, fifties, or sixties. There are now even documented cases in the age groups of the twenties and thirties! What are we to do with so many afflicted? It is good to become informed. There are standard "markers" or milestones that sufferers reach, but they do not always appear in the same order. Everyone is unique. Therefore, we would have to take it one day at a time and troubleshoot each milestone as it arose, while trying to prepare as much as the disease would allow.

Mom continued to function with increased supervision for a couple of years. She still drove herself to the grocery store and to the hairdresser, but we were beginning to question her driving abilities. One day, she encountered a detour on her way home from the hairdresser which was only two miles away from home. She became lost, but eventually found her way back. This episode frightened her to the point that she surrendered her car keys (thank goodness) and made her own decision that her driving days were over. The next year, she tripped on her hallway carpet and broke her arm. Fortunately, I was there at the time and was able to call 911 for help. After that, I arranged for her to wear an automated lifeline button that would call 911 for her when she pressed the button for assistance. However, the problem with an emergency button for AD patients is their failure to remember what the button is for, or they will even forget that they are wearing it.

It took the broken arm for her to grudgingly allow a part-time caregiver to come in to help her. It is very beneficial to utilize a caregiver you can trust. It would have been a good idea to try to find one in advance of needing one, if that is possible. Caregiving agencies are a good source when you need them. They work well for some people, and for others, they are good in a pinch. However, in our situation, I found they had scheduling problems and staffing problems and when caregivers did not show up, I would only learn of their absence by chance afterward, because Mom was not able to tell me. In addition, Mom was very uncomfortable with the parade of different caregivers, and she had personality conflicts with a few. It would have been ideal to enlist a family member who could help out on a regular basis, but we had no one able to assist at this time, so we opted for a privately-hired caregiver. After trying several, I found Julie —who was efficient, organized, and kind. My mother loved her.

About the same time that Mom broke her arm, I noticed she was writing an overabundance of checks for her condo-association dues, so we determined it was now time for me to assume the function of paying her bills. One day, she forgot to shut off a burner on the stove and scorched her teapot. So for her safety, our solution was to trip the fuse to her stove so it couldn't be turned on, and she was never the wiser. We arranged for Meals on Wheels to deliver meals to her door.

Apparently, there is a formal classification system that health professionals use to determine the level of function a person has. You do not have the capacity for basic physical independence if you lack the eight "activities of daily living" (ADL) which include: using the toilet, eating, dressing, bathing, grooming, getting out of bed, getting out of a chair, and walking, all without assistance. (Mom has no difficulty performing these activities at this time.) Additionally, you do not have the capacity to live safely on your own if you can no longer perform the "instrumental activities of daily living" (IADL) which include: preparing your own food, maintaining your housekeeping, doing your laundry, managing your medications, making phone calls, traveling on your own, or handling your finances. (Mom is having difficulties managing some of these items). The time had come, and in fact, was now overdue, to move her out of her condo to a safer environment. I discussed with my sisters the possibility of moving her to an assisted living home where she might be safer, but the day we arrived at her condo to take her on a tour of the homes, she stubbornly kicked up the footrest on her recliner, leaned back, and seemed to plant herself, refusing to budge. It is formidable to forfeit your independence. It seems that with each memory that goes, there also goes another function, another purpose, another role. I tried to win small battles against the disease by assuring Mom that she was useful, needed, and loved. Even while having to remove some of her responsibilities, it was good to give her other responsibilities she could handle so she would feel useful.

Seven years after Mom's original diagnosis, she underwent back surgery, but the type of anesthetic used left her completely and utterly disoriented. For several weeks, my sisters and I would need to be her constant companions, taking turns sleeping at her condo since she could not be left alone. She could no longer perform the IADL and, in fact, could not even perform the ADL without assistance. Our options had now narrowed considerably, and the only option available was for her to move to an assisted living home. Health insurance does not cover assisted living home costs.

The hospitality manager at the assisted living home we chose knew my mother's diagnosis, and she wooed us with promises that Mom could have her own apartment on the "independent" side of the home, and when she needed more care, she could move to the "assisted" side of the home. The "independent" apartment cost would be between two thousand and three thousand dollars per month, and yes, all of her needs would be taken care of. The "assisted" costs would be more depending on the size of the apartment and the level of care, but we were assured they would care for her, and she could stay there until the very end.

It took a couple of months before some, but not all, of the functional memory she lost from the anesthetic had returned, and she could once again perform most of the activities of daily living. We found her a nice two-bedroom apartment on the "independent" side of the home. The second bedroom would be useful if she needed someone to stay with her. This was one of the few facilities where she was allowed to take her cat with her. Julie and I would visit her there a few times a week to ensure Mom was receiving the care she needed. This home experienced a multitude of frequent staff changes at all levels, which proved to be a challenge for me in coordinating care and medications, but Mom was quite comfortable there for about three years.

There now came a point in time where Mom required more supervision and care, so the staff at the home suggested Mom move to the "assisted" side. This was a studio apartment and quite smaller than the previous one.

These were all the milestone occasions requiring life-and-death decisions that resulted from the gradual, incessant pilfering of her mind. As her primary caregiver, I had to be there every step of the way, witnessing, investigating, advocating, and chasing the thief who was looting my mother's life, and then pick up the pieces as I labored along that path. So many times, it seemed I was always following behind, never ever getting ahead of its next move, because this bandit wanted to call the shots.

I was very disappointed with the care she received on the "assisted living" side of the home. The aides seemed short-staffed, so their visits were rushed and shoddy, overlooking many basic functions of care. She actually received better hands-on care on the "independent" side. One of the aides had been charged by the police for stealing a resident's credit cards. I was advised to remove Mom's wedding ring and other jewelry and take them home. Mom had not even been in the assisted living side of the home one year before she began to wander outside of her apartment and was not able to find her way back. One staff member told me about a door mat with an alarm they could put outside her door so they would know when she wandered out, but we never received that mat. Higher-level staff now tell me they are not a memory care lock-down facility, and so for her safety, we would have to move her out. Whatever happened to the promise that she could stay there until the end? Moving is very hard on AD patients. Each move sets them back and causes them to lose memory functions that will probably not return.

Although there are still some nations and cultures where it is assumed that the elderly will live with their family members, and many households are multi-generational, our country has slowly moved away from this scenario. There are many reasons for this change, but it seems that, in our country, our first train of thought is always to find a facility that can provide the knowledge and services to care for such people. This was certainly the way I was thinking. My husband, Jim and I toured several memory care facilities, becoming very discouraged to find the cost was staggering, and insurance offers no benefits for these facilities, either. In our part of the nation, memory care facilities cost between four thousand and eleven thousand dollars per month, depending on the level of care needed. Social Security checks do not even put a dent in this magnitude of cost.

Now it just so happens that within the next two months, I was retiring from my position as a county Veterans benefits counselor. In my career, I assisted many Veterans and their widows file for pension or compensation benefits to help defray the cost of assisted living and caregiver services. These benefits could even defray the costs of caring for your loved one in your home. This is a wonderful benefit available for Veterans and their widows, and more and more people are learning about this benefit. In our situation, however, neither of my parents were Veterans, so Mom was not eligible to receive that assistance.

It is now nearly eleven years after Mom's original AD diagnosis, and a momentous question looms on the horizon. She is ninety years old. Where is she to go? I was facing an inner struggle. I greatly feared what was becoming my only option. God has been with me for every step and for every decision, so it was only natural for me to turn to Him to ask my question. He responded to me loudly and clearly, and the conversation went something like this: "Move her in with you". This was not a still, small voice, or a gentle urging; it was unmistakable—a booming directive. For several days I wrestled (like Jacob wrestled with Him?), arguing "But she can't manage steps and our guest rooms are upstairs and downstairs". God replied, "Give her your master's bedroom on the main floor". I continued to argue, "What about my sisters? Why can't she move in with them?" God stated, "I didn't call them. I called you." It is tempting when we are faced with an onerous decision to expect others to help us or to "do their part", but we have to be very careful of the expectations we place on others because that can lead to our resentment and disappointment. What we expect from someone may not be God's plan for that person. Such resentment and disappointment are yet other reasons that many families are ripped apart, causing lifelong battles and hardships. God also knew that I had concerns on how this move would affect my marriage, but this much wiser power carefully laid the foundation for every flawless detail to fall into place. He gave Jim the grace to accept our new arrangement without a flinch.

I have no medical training or experience, and I certainly had fear that I would not be up to the task. Caregiver handbooks are helpful to teach the mechanics of caring for the physical body, seminars are helpful to teach about enlisting help and other resources, but no one could tell me what to expect or how to handle the heart-wrenching grief of watching her further decline on a daily basis, opening myself up to such an emotional roller coaster. I was even naïve to the type of death we would have to face. I had to trust that God knew what he was doing, because I certainly didn't. I couldn't stop it any more than I could halt a freight train barreling down the track to its next stop--my front door.

Julie would assist us with caregiving a couple half days a week, and my friend, Jeanne, would assist on Saturdays so Jim and I could have our "date night". I had a couple telephone numbers for back-up caregivers. I was prepared as much as I could expect to be with not knowing what to expect. The very next day after I retired from the county, my mother (who now doesn't know me from Adam) is to move in with us. What follows is our final journey through the darkest gully in the valley, the daily account of the remaining life we share together, my mom, myself, and the thief, with God's rod and staff leading the way.

PART 2

FULFILLING THE PROMISE

1

The last memory I had of my mom and dad's life together was in late September 2001. Jim and I took them to a local cider mill in the quaint town of Parshallville, Michigan that they had never visited before. The five-story mill was built in 1869 with barn wood, now blackened with age. It is one of the few remaining water-powered mills in Michigan. Its towering wheel is still churning water traveling down North Ore Creek, just the other side of the dam from the mill pond. What a beautiful autumn day. The gold, red, and orange leaves were crunching under our feet as we walked across the bridge to approach the mill from the parking lot.

When we emerged from the mill a short time later with our cider and a bag of donuts in hand, the bees were buzzing, drawn by the sweet smell of the cider in our cups. Daddy told me he loved the cider mill and planned to bring my mother back again. At one point, he took me aside and said that my mom was "losing it". He said she misplaced her keys and blamed him for hiding them. I laughed and dismissed it as part of the natural aging process. He also told me that their routine of golfing three times a week for more than thirty years had come to an end. They just golfed for the last time that week.

I couldn't believe what I was hearing. I questioned why, arguing that they should keep golfing for the exercise. My parents' golfing defined them for me. As long as they were golfing, I had two viable, healthy parents that were still enjoying life. He didn't give me an answer, so I will never know why. Just a little more than one month later, he was gone.

[Journal Entries]

April 6, 2013

After retiring from my job yesterday, and a fitful sleep last night, this monumental day dawned earlier than usual. Jim and I had already moved our belongings out of our master's suite and prepared it for Mom. The appropriate doors have locks or alarms, and the stage is set. Laurie and her twin daughters, Stefanie and Stacy, volunteered to help. Our neighbors are good friends (more like family when we need them), and today, our caravan of trucks, SUV's, cars, and a trailer arrived at the assisted living home in the morning. With so much help, Mom's apartment was packed and loaded in no more than an hour. Another two hours and our master's suite was her new home. My daughter-in-law, Wendi, could now bring Mom from their house, where she was safely tucked away from the chaos and commotion. Alzheimer's patients can become agitated with commotion. With my caregivers in place, and somehow, with God's help and direction, this new season in our lives is falling smoothly into place. In fact, it feels very much like a *blessing*. I look forward to the time we will have together.

Mom has no memory of our life together, but she enjoys hearing me tell her of it. As a young adult, I never, for the life of me, could visualize having to help my mother dress, or attend to her other most basic needs. But a few years back, when she sensed my discomfort, and with wisdom beyond my years, she made the simple statement, "I don't have anything you don't have". Wow, she was still teaching me. I should have been easing her discomfort, yet, she was easing mine. From that point on, I relaxed, knowing all would be okay. Whatever bridge we had to cross, we would cross it together.

The lines of relationship have become blurred. I don't know exactly when it happened, but I guess it was a gradual transition. Just like a child slowly grows to adulthood, my mother has gradually become my child. I don't look at it as a bad thing, but more as a link in a cycle—like life has come around full-circle. She took care of me when I couldn't take care of myself, and now it is my time to take care of her when she cannot take care of herself.

The last few weeks I tried to prepare her for the move. I would tell her, "You're going to move in with me".

Then she would brighten and say, "Oh really? I would really like that. That is so nice of you." Five minutes later, we would have the same conversation. However, the tone of her response was always the same; she was happy. Today was a long day for her. In the late afternoon she said, "Are you going to take me home now?"

To which I responded, "You are home. Our home is now your home."

And then she would smile and say, "Oh really?"

We placed motion detectors in her room and the corresponding alarm sounds in my bedroom when she opens her door. She opened it twice tonight. I had to reassure her and tuck her back into bed. "Sleep tight and sweet dreams." This has a familiar ring to it. She would say it to me a long time ago; more role reversal. It is a strange and new relationship, to be sure, but one that we've grown respectively comfortable with. Our goal with AD patients should be to keep them happy, comfortable, and safe. There was a time in my life when I dreaded ever having to be in this position, but the fear is gone; I am not alone. God orchestrated this transition, and He will see us through.

April 9, 2013

The last couple of days passed with much busyness—a flurry of organizing. Today we had errands to run. During the first years of Mom's Alzheimer's, when she still lived in her condo, I took her to the library as a regular outing because she loved to read. (Reading is a great brain exercise.) She would pick out about eight mystery novels (her favorite genre) and read them all. Her example revived my love for reading and soon I was choosing seven or eight books, as well. In fact, we became so weighted down with books, I purchased luggage on wheels to take them back and forth. Reading is a great stress release for me. Today we went to the library together for the first time in about a year. A year ago, we found she lost the ability to understand what she was reading and we had to go searching for her library books that she would leave strewn in various places around her assisted living home. For this visit, I went straight to the children's section and got her a story book. When we returned home, she seemed eager to read it to me, although she missed several words. It will still be a good brain exercise for her.

April 11, 2013

Mom is very sweet these days. She tries to help, so I try to allow her to carry her dishes to the kitchen. At this stage in the disease, folding anything is a favorite pastime, so I had her fold the towels, and she did a really good job. This morning, when I took her dentures out of the soak and handed them to her, she didn't remember where they should go and put them on her nose. It was funny, but also sad. I've learned this week that she can no longer be left in a room alone for too long because she will go wandering. Today I took a shower, and twenty minutes later when I emerged, she was rattling around in the kitchen. When I investigated, to my horror, she had eaten some raw hamburger that was defrosting on the counter. These are real eye-opening events for me. Today was the very first day since coming to live here that she did not say, "Are you going to take me home now?" I will now take my showers before I get her out of bed in the morning.

April 12, 2013

Confusion is the word of the day. This morning, I took Mom into the bathroom to relieve herself, and she asked if she should go in the tub, then asked if she should go in the shower. Then as I was pointing out the toilet, I noticed that she had urinated in the wastebasket sometime during the night. How on earth could she even maneuver herself to do that?

It has been rainy and cold all week—and it is supposed to snow tonight. I found out yesterday that my cat has cancer with a life expectancy of one month. This cat loves sitting on Mom's lap, purring almost in a trance as Mom repeatedly strokes her back. Since Mom recently lost her cat, Jack, it seems these two are now soothing each other like kindred souls. It is a serene picture, but one that could end very soon.

April 14, 2013

The weekend was a good one. Two caregivers came yesterday, one for morning and one for afternoon. It went very well. Today we went out for breakfast and then the grocery store. I let Mom push the cart both for the exercise and for support for walking. Her tendency was to move fast, so I walked in front of the cart, thinking it would slow her down,—Wrong–she rammed the cart into my ankle. No serious damage done, but, boy, did that hurt. Suffice it to say, I will no longer walk in front of the cart. Shortly after that, we went to church together.

This afternoon we played the card game that I played as a child—war. This was another great brain exercise for her. She read me the numbers on the cards, and then I asked her which number was higher. She improved reading the numbers on the cards and always knew which was higher. She usually knew which one of us won the hand when I asked her. She kept on trying—was a little disappointed when she missed knowing a number, but did not grow frustrated, and I encouraged her with how good she was doing. She ate a good dinner of Crockpot chicken, mashed potatoes, and peas. We had chocolate cake for dessert. She really enjoyed that, and I really enjoyed her company. The sun set on a delightful day. My mom is teaching me so much, to be patient and more loving, unintentionally teaching me lessons that I wasn't so good at learning in my childhood.

April 15, 2013

I did some cleaning this morning and then checked the weather forecast. With thunderstorms predicted the rest of the week, it looked like this afternoon would be the best time to golf, so I took the plunge and made a tee time. This was a first for me, to golf solo and take Mom for company. Who knows, she may even want to putt. I know the rules; I can do this. Mom and Dad golfed for thirty years together after retirement, and I know Mom loved it. I bundled her up, and we set out. Despite my poor game, we laughed, the sun came out and it was tranquil.

A few times, I heard Mom repeat, "I used to do this. This is familiar to me." These were the best structured sentences I'd heard from her in quite a while. When I asked if she wanted to putt, she refused, saying she hadn't done that in a long time. I gave her a couple opportunities, but she continued to decline the offers. It didn't matter. She enjoyed riding in the cart, and she enjoyed the conversation; it was stimulating to her. Besides, she was getting fresh air and was not stuck in front of the television. It was a good day.

April 17, 2013

A day in the life of a caregiver: Unless someone is a caregiver, there is no way to know how much time is involved. Today was a perfect example. This morning, after getting her out of bed, washed, brushed, and dressed, and given breakfast and medications, I threw in a load of her laundry, and then I made phone calls. I called the dermatologist and made an appointment. I then called her primary doctor to make an appointment and request a blood-draw requisition. I called the financial planner to set up an IRA for Mom's lump-sum pension buy-out. He advised of the paperwork needed to set it up (which I had to gather), as well as a needed Michigan ID. Since Mom's driver's license had expired, I called the secretary of state to find out what was needed to obtain the ID, and I was put on hold for twenty minutes. I then had to gather those items. I gave Mom lunch and got her ready, and we went to the secretary of state. When we walked in the door of the secretary of state, we took no. 48 and right away heard the clerk call the next number to be waited on, no. 13. We ended up being there for an hour. When we arrived home, I had to read the buy-out contract, which took about half an hour, then scan and e-mail information to the financial advisor. During this time on the computer, I had to get up and check on Mom every ten minutes because that was the time limit before she would get up and wander, going into the kitchen and start rooting about, eating food and moving papers around. I then began to prepare dinner.

Around 6:00 p.m., the pharmacy called to announce Mom's medications would be delivered in two hours, and then a caregiver called to advise she could not care for Mom during Wendi's upcoming surprise birthday party, so I will have to find someone else or take her with us. After dinner, Mom repeatedly said she wanted to go to bed. I put her off for a bit, trying to keep her occupied, fearing if she went to bed too early, she would not sleep through the night. However, a good lesson to learn is that you do not argue with an AD patient. Sometimes it works just to change the subject, but this night, she just wanted to go to bed. The medications were delivered at 8:00 p.m., and now I could don my pajamas and have some time to myself, so long as she does not set off the alarm. Caring for mom is not so difficult; but what I find more challenging, is trying to get everything else done *while* caring for her.

April 19, 2013

It was a pretty good day today. Julie came and took Mom to the hairdresser after giving her a shower. My mother used to knit and crochet countless afghans, baby layettes, sweaters, hats, mittens, doilies, anything she could find, and she did absolutely beautiful work. Today I rolled a ball of yarn and put some stitches on a needle, asking if she wanted to try knitting a little bit, but she said, "No, maybe tomorrow".

Yesterday she tried to color a picture but did not quite understand what she was doing, nor could she associate what color the subjects should be, like turtles are green. She did not want to finish it. It does not accomplish anything if she grows frustrated, so I try to keep things fun, and when she doesn't want to do it anymore, we stop. Sometimes I can see her thinking so hard, prompted by functions she used to have, trying to remember what she used to do. I think sometimes she doesn't want to try things she used to do because she fears failing. Tonight, we watched "The Money Pit" on television, and we laughed together. It was good.

April 21, 2013

I am weary after a long day. We went out for breakfast, as has been our habit on Sundays for at least twelve years now. Mom can still cut her pancakes with her fork, but can no longer cut the meat. I cut up most foods for her. We went to church so she could take communion. It took a lot of instruction. I always peek to see if she could still mouth along to the "Lord's Prayer" like she could in the not-too-distant past, but not today; I only saw a blank look.

This afternoon, I went upstairs for a few minutes and she wandered to the kitchen and then grabbed a cupcake. The second time she wandered to the cupcakes, I had to say she should not eat that because I was preparing a large dinner with apple pie for dessert. She seemed restless. She looked into the china cabinet today and said, "Leslie, Laurie, and Ronnie".

I said, "Yes, your daughters, what about them?"

She repeated "Leslie, Laurie, and Ronnie," and then she looked at a clock and the other items in the china cabinet, reached out, but then withdrew her hand and grew a little frustrated. I so much wanted to know what she was thinking—a memory she was desperately trying to recapture. This was the first time she recited her children's names in a long, long time.

I pointed to the clock and said, "Do you remember, that is your twenty-fifth-anniversary clock?"

She said, "Oh really?" seeming genuinely happy at the thought.

During the day today, she also mentioned her three brothers and how they looked out for her and would question her whenever they saw her with a guy, mostly to warn her away from him. I asked her if they did that when she started dating Daddy.

She said, "No, they liked him." She had a smile on her face when she said Daddy was a really good man. Later on when we were watching a golf tournament on television, she said, "I used to really like doing that".

Jim said, "You were very, very good at it".

She responded, "My brothers taught me."

I never knew this. It seems as if this disease steals the top layer of memories first, and then works its way down the layers, until the only memories left are of childhood. She seems to be somewhere in her early twenties or teenage years at this point. I want to capture and hold all those memories if I can.

She wanted to go to bed at 7:00 p.m. At 9:00 p.m., the alarm sounded as she opened her door. I found her up and trying to peer out her window in the dark, so I turned on the light and asked what was wrong, but she said she didn't know. She said she heard something and thought something was wrong and she just doesn't know what it was. I had to reassure her that everything was all right. Nothing was wrong. I tucked her into bed, told her I loved her and to "sleep tight".

She looked up at me and said, "I appreciate everything you do for me."

How bitter sweet. It warms my heart that she knows enough to be appreciative of me, but she appreciates me as her caregiver; the memory of me being her daughter was stolen away quite some time ago.

April 22, 2013

Up and down—running to and fro—it is hard to keep up with Mom. It seemed every five minutes she was up and headed into the kitchen. She got herself a cupcake and then got into the apple pie. She wanted an English muffin, and then she wanted another one five minutes later because she did not remember just eating one. I gave her animal crackers and strawberries and graham crackers. After all that, she looked at me and said, "How come I can't get anything to eat in this place?"

I try to remind her gently of what she has eaten and then say, "I'm making a big dinner, and you won't eat your dinner if you eat now," (I may be echoing what she used to say to me in my childhood), but you have to be on your toes to keep up with her. Maybe I'll drop a few pounds with all this activity.

April 25, 2013

After lunch today, Mom complained that her thigh hurt, "like it's never hurt before". It did not abate, and I started thinking, maybe it could be a blood clot or something serious. Of course, this scared me, so I took her to the ER. We were there a total of two and a half hours, during which time they took X-rays, an ultrasound, and urine sample. She absolutely hated the time waiting for results. Over and over she would say, "What's taking them so long? Where is everyone? Isn't anyone coming? If someone doesn't come soon, I'm just going to get up and leave. Why am I here anyway?" Then the whole diatribe would be repeated, over and over.

In order to calm her, my response would be, "It won't be much longer. We have to make sure you're okay. Your leg hurt, remember? I'd rather be safe than sorry, so you're getting checked out. If we aren't sitting here, we'd just be sitting someplace else anyway." But then she would not remember any of those things that I said, and it would begin all over again. Finally, the nurse practitioner (a doctor never did come to see us) told us the X-rays were okay—no blood clot on ultrasound, but they did find an urinary-tract infection (that explains a lot). UTI's can cause mental confusion. She gave us a prescription for antibiotics and sent us on our way. I think they were glad to see us go.

April 28, 2013

We went to breakfast and church this morning. It feels like we are settling into a routine of sorts, although each day brings its own surprises. It seems the "good" days, where she seems lucid, are fewer and further between. Sadly, I am growing accustomed to her blank stare. She cannot comprehend what she watches on television, nor is she able to follow a story line. It is common for her to say, "Why are they doing that?" Also, when she speaks, she normally confuses the name of something for something else, like when she saw an elephant and called it a cat, or she'll just say, "You know, those *things*". Most often, she just grows frustrated and says, "Oh, never mind". I try to play along like I know what she's trying to say to prevent her frustration, or I try to find the words for her. It is sad to see her try so hard to communicate, only to give up in frustration.

This afternoon, I saw her looking at family photographs hanging on the wall. I pointed to her senior class photo and said, "Do you know who that is?"

"No".

"That's you."

She chuckled and said, "It doesn't look like me".

I pointed to her children and said, "Do you know who they are?"

"No".

"They are your children, Leslie, Laurie and that's me, Ronnie, when I was little."

"Oh, really?"

"Do you know who I am?"

"No".

"I'm your daughter, Ronnie".

Then she reverted to her most common phrase, "You know it's funny how you forget things sometimes". It is almost like she is fighting the disease with everything she has. I can see in her eyes she knows something is wrong, but doesn't know how to change it. I could see her searching my face to see if she could pull up some recognition, some memory, but any memory of our sixty-year history has been erased, gone or buried beneath tangles of brain plaque. This is an insidious disease. I'm somewhat emotional today. It's been a long, long road.

April 30, 2013

I got Mom up from bed an hour early this morning to take her with us for Jim's medical procedure. She had oatmeal, cinnamon raisin toast, and a sausage link before we left; and a Rice Krispies bar at the hospital. She was restless when we got home and wouldn't sit down. She continued to hunt for any food she could eat. I gave her an egg-salad sandwich and half an apple for lunch. After lunch, she had animal crackers and still wouldn't sit down, proceeding to eat two or three donut holes. Then, as she started complaining about her leg hurting again, she said she wanted to go to bed, so she laid down for a nap.

I got her up two hours later, and surprisingly, she then sat in the rocking chair for an entire movie. She had a snack, and after we ate dinner at 6:00 p.m., she wanted to go to bed again. I will give her the last of her medications at 9:00 p.m. I am beginning to believe that maybe she just needs more sleep. We didn't get our walk today because it was raining, and then after dinner when I asked if she wanted to walk, she said she just wanted to go to bed. I'm just trying to make sense of it. I am no doctor. Tomorrow we're going to her primary doctor's office for a follow up on the UTI. I plan to mention the restlessness and wandering. Although I suspect to be told that those are typical symptoms of Alzheimer's, maybe they can give me some solution, and also a remedy for the leg pain. I need some help with this. This wandering is wearing me out. Even if I put all the food away, she would just grow agitated looking for something to eat. I think I'll try letting her take a daily nap. Maybe this is what she needs.

2

I have fond memories of golfing with my parents. For sixteen years Mom and Dad had an annual membership to a golf course and Jim and I golfed with them there several times. Ironically, the golf course was later sold to build medical facilities, including the very same assisted living home where she would later reside for four years. Her first apartment there overlooked a pond encircled with a paved golf cart path, where we strolled and recanted whatever golfing memories we could muster.

My dad loved to give me golf lessons, and most often today, when I hit the ball off the fairway, I can still hear him say, "Well, that went right where you were aiming". I could use some of those lessons now. My mother could not drive the ball a great distance, but she was consistently straight as an arrow. She drove the ball to land in the same place every time. Her other shots were just as consistent and pretty close to target. They were both very good golfers, and I know they relished the times we were able to join them. I now wish we would have done it more often.

[Journal Entries]

May 8, 2013

Naps don't work. (At least they didn't work today.) I ask if she wants to take one, but she says "No".

However, she wants to go to bed about 4:00 p.m., and I have to say we're going to eat dinner soon, so it would be best to wait a bit. Then right after dinner, she says, "Can't I go upstairs to my room now?" (Her room is on the main floor.) She has a very difficult time trying to articulate what she is thinking, and then she gets frustrated. Earlier today, we did yoga together to a yoga DVD. Of course, her movement was very limited, but the stretching and deep breathing will help her to become more flexible. In fact, during our walk down the street today, it was the first time she did not complain about her back hurting. I would like to do yoga with her two to three times per week. It may prevent a fall. She really tried to do everything I asked of her and I praised her at every twist and turn and bend. God bless her.

Tonight, after getting her ready for bed, she said she was afraid, and I said, "Of what?" She said, "Of waking up here," and "Where is everybody?"

I said, "You're not at the assisted living home. You've lived here a month now. This is your home now. There's nothing to be afraid of". I tried to reassure her. I wish so much to know what was troubling her. Even when a child is having a nightmare, you know how to comfort them.

She put her hands over her face and said, "I'm just not ready for this". As I sat there with her, in my heart, I silently agreed with her.

May 10, 2013

Even though Julie was here this morning and she took Mom out to get Mom's hair done, by 1:30 p.m., Mom was bored again. This has become the pattern: the television is on a station she would normally like, but she can't stay focused on it; she heaves a big disgusted sigh, starts looking around, she "tsks-tsks" a few times, and says she wants to go to bed. If I say we're going to eat dinner in a little while, does she want to take a nap, she says "no". Then she starts to wander around until she finally sits down ten to twenty minutes later and says, "I want to go home now".

By 4:00 p.m. she had made these comments so many times, I finally said it was okay for her to go to bed. After a one-hour nap, I woke her up to eat dinner, and she wanted to go right back to bed after dinner. At this point, she is in her bed twelve to thirteen hours a day. She seems to require constant entertainment and my constant attention, but I have other responsibilities to take care of. I thought the routine was working pretty well, but she grows more and more restless. Her demands are wearing me thin. God, help me never to run out of patience, to find activities to keep her busy, and to give me the energy to care for her.

May 12, 2013

It's Mother's Day, and I am so glad I still have my mom. I see snippets of who she used to be when I look into her eyes. Or maybe, I'm just picturing her as she used to be before all her memories were heisted. We all went to breakfast, then Mom and I went to church. My son, Jeff, daughter-in-law Wendi and our grandson, Chase, were at church. At 2:00 p.m., we went to Jeff and Wendi's house to celebrate Mother's Day, as well as Wendi's fortieth birthday. Mom smiled a lot. She conversed somewhat.

I noticed she got up out of her chair and wandered into the dining room, so I asked her where she was going, and she said "to my room". I had to tell her she had no room there, but that Jeff was fixing dinner for us and we would be eating soon. This scenario occurred twice more before we actually sat down to eat. I think this is the first time Wendi's parents had seen Mom so confused. She continued to grow restless, so shortly after dinner, we had to leave. Mom went to bed when we got home at 7:00 p.m.

Last week, I spoke to my son, Roger (who worked as a certified nursing assistant), and he told me he felt bad because he knew what was ahead for me to deal with. I didn't ask him what was ahead, because all I have strength for right now is to take one day at a time. God says that His strength is sufficient. Therefore, I must lean on His strength and love to equip me with what I need, and His timing will be perfect.

May 15, 2013

It is a time of for adjustment for Mom, also for everyone else in the family. She continues to be confused about her surroundings. She sleeps about twelve hours a day and still wanders —mostly into the kitchen looking for food. Sometimes her attitude becomes somewhat demanding, rather strong-willed. Now, I recall her always having a tendency toward this character trait, (which, historically, usually rubs me the wrong way). I must remember to keep it simple and keep the mood light.

She really responds to kindness. When I get her ready for bed, she says, "You're nice". She has no memory of me or any of our life together, so I grieve the loss. Sometimes I mention an occasion or a vacation we took, and she just stares at me with that vacant look, like she's searching her brain for it, but it really makes no sense to her. She is confusing her words. She wants to communicate, but the sentence comes out in such a jumble of words, it is impossible to decipher her intent. She grows restless watching television because she cannot comprehend what is being said.

May 16, 2013

We lost our cable television this morning, so I put on my wedding DVD. I pointed to the screen and asked Mom if she recognized that person (me). She said, "She looks familiar". I told her that was me at my wedding. I asked if she recognized that girl with me and she said, "No".

I said, "That was Leslie".

"Oh really?"

Then when Daddy came on, she did not say a word. There was no sign of recognition.

As he danced the father/daughter dance with me, I said, "He loved to dance, he was such a good dancer", but she did not say a word. She was half of this couple who took ballroom dancing decades earlier. She had loved to dance. Her expression was placid, which gave me the feeling she more feared saying the wrong thing just because she felt I was expecting her to say something.

She didn't recognize herself. She showed slight recognition of her brother, Bud, but it was fleeting. Tonight, Jim and I took her to the driving range and set her up in a chair in the shade while we drove golf balls.

Several times, she said, "I used to do that all the time", and she was happy. That memory unburied itself and almost surprised her that she recalled golfing. These recollections are very few and far between these days, but it is good to get her out of the house and stimulate her mind with good memories. It was a beautiful sunset tonight with warm colors of orange and pink.

May 18, 2013

Tonight, when Mom got in bed, she looked right at me and said, "I love you". I really got the impression that she knew who I was when she said it. Just for her to remember those words and say them in the proper sequence, at a time when the vast majority of her conversation is garbled and mostly senseless, is a miracle. It's as if when she speaks out of her spirit, the words are clear and heartfelt full sentences, but when her diseased brain is trying to speak, her words are mostly mumbled, unintelligible sounds. I will cherish those "spirit" sentences in the inner sanctum of my heart, to draw upon during the coming wearisome days when I will need to remember.

May 19, 2013

It was a very busy day—out to breakfast, to church, and to Chase's football game in the afternoon. Afterwards, we went to get ice cream. Mom very much enjoyed the football game, and even jokingly said she would like to go out and join them play. Walking back to the car was quite a distance, and on a decline, so I had to hold onto her tightly to prevent a tumble. She kept leaning way forward and could hardly pick up her feet. This is what is typically known as the "Alzheimer's shuffle". I could feel the potential for a fall, so we need to find an alternative so we can continue to attend the football games and other functions. The highlight of the day was at the time of good-bye.

Chase went over to get a hug from Mom, and she said, "I love you".

Chase smiled and said, "I love you, too".

It warmed my heart to see this exchange between a great-grandma and her great-grandson.

May 20, 2013

We celebrated Mom's ninety-first birthday tonight since everyone else had commitments later in the week. Before the family arrived, Mom was very restless and wandering around, very irritated that we wouldn't get to eat dinner until 6:00 p.m., saying, "Well, I'll just go to bed then".

It was all I could do to keep her occupied and happy, and, of course, it did not help that she picked up a television remote and hit the wrong button. I could not get the cable back on. When the family finally arrived between 4:00 p.m. and 5:00 p.m., she seemed more content. Mom sat outside and had a good time watching Chase get a little bit crazy on his slip and slide. Due to snacking before dinner, she just picked at her shish-ke-bobs. Chase had to help her blow out the candles on her cake, but she sure enjoyed eating it. We had to repeatedly remind her it was her birthday. We again watched our wedding DVD, with the family this time, and Mom made no recognition, even when she and Daddy were doing a marvelous swing dance.

Wendi turned to me and said, "She doesn't know who he is, does she?" I sadly shook my head, no. Our birthday photograph today will picture a happy and whole family celebrating a ninety-first birthday, but even though she is there physically, she is not mentally. It may almost sound cruel to mention what a vacant, hollow look there is to her eyes. I search her face for a flicker of memory of the life we have shared, but there is none to be found. She doesn't recognize herself, her husband, or her children. She is slipping away.

May 21, 2013

Today was cleaning day for me—translating to "boredom

day" for Mom. This results in irritation and demands to "do something" or wandering and incessant grazing, as well as repeating, "I'm just going to go to bed".

Today when she said it once again at 3:00 p.m., I simply said, "Okay".

She went. I got her up at 5:00 p.m. when dinner was ready, and she was ready to go back to bed by 6:30 p.m. It is becoming obvious that this is my challenge—to keep focused—to remember that she does not remember anything more than ten seconds before. To try to assuage her demands, maybe I'll seek some help on how to do this before my patience wears thin.

May 23, 2013

Leslie and Laurie called to wish Mom a happy birthday. Phone conversations are very short these days. Her hearing is suffering some loss. Everything I say to her has to be repeated—is it hearing, or is it loss of comprehension? Maybe it's a little of both. When I take her to the doctor, I make sure they clean the wax out of her ears, because ear wax can affect her hearing. We also have ear wash that we use at home.

To get her out of the house, I took her to the cinema today to see "The Great Gatsby". My thought was that she may have some recognition of the era and clothes. She attempted to take the top off her Pepsi cup twice, and I had to teach her how to use the straw. Halfway through the movie, she leaned over and said, "I want to go home now".

I told her the movie wasn't over yet, we still need to see the end. For the next twenty minutes, she grew more restless and then "tsked" and gave a huge sigh. This happened three or four more times, so I acquiesced, and we left. It is obvious she has a short attention span with little or no comprehension even at the movie theater. She cannot follow the story line.

I recall when my parents took me to the movies as a kid, I would always ask, "Why are they doing that?" or "What do they mean by that?" Boy, have the tables now turned. Now Mom asks me those same questions. Sometimes it seems I would not mind returning to the innocence of my youth. Ignorance is bliss, as they say. I suppose dementia is one way to return to that innocence, but it is a hard way to go. Jesus said we should all be as little children. That means trusting completely in Him, just as we trusted as little children. My joy and my strength are in Him. Tomorrow we will begin assembling a scrapbook of her life. I think we will call it her life book.

May 27, 2013

Today is Memorial Day. Julie was here this morning, so Jim and I took the opportunity to go golfing and had a nice time off by ourselves. When we got home, at 1:00 p.m., Mom began to say she wanted to go to bed. At 2:00 p.m., she went to her room and donned some pajamas with some street clothes on top. A half-hour later, she began folding the clothes in her closet. I helped her to dress again, and we went out to sit with the neighbors. I think she gets bored quite easily, and this can cause restlessness. Sometimes we have to be creative and redirect her activities. She enjoys being with other people, as long as the gathering is small. I made hot tea for her since it was quite chilly outside.

Sometimes her restlessness, pacing, and grazing makes me weary. I suppose it would be honest to say I grow resentful at times of having this responsibility of keeping her entertained, occupied, and just safe. But I am reminded of the Bible story of Noah's drunkenness when one of his sons was disrespectful, yet the other son respected him and covered his shame reverently. God reminded me that I should respect my mother that much and more, because it is not her fault she has an illness.

May 28, 2013

It is another cleaning day here already. I rose to the challenge of her boredom. When Mom began to pace and wonder what she was supposed to do, I pulled some towels out of the closet and had her refold them. As the morning progressed, I had her fold several loads of laundry. She is also becoming adept at drying the dishes. She appears to thrive when she accomplishes something.

Today she asked me, "Do you live close to here?" This afternoon, I prepared the family tree and title page for her life book. A photo of her at age sixteen is on the title page, but when I showed it to her, she said, "That is not me".

I suppose when I look at photos of myself as a child, if I did not know from my memory that those photos were of me, I would not recognize them, either. At this point, Mom lives in the moment. She exhibited a snippet of memory today when we were discussing ice skating, and I said that I knew she used to love to ice skate. She said, "My brothers taught me how to skate". Today was a good day.

May 29, 2013

It was time for Mom's six-month checkup today. Her pulse has been lower lately. The doctor said this was probably caused by the blood pressure medicines she is taking, but the doctor did not want to alter her medications since they are keeping her blood pressure under control. She did stop the cholesterol medicine, however. I love our doctor. She is very caring, very knowledgeable, and she likes to laugh. We discussed Mom's wandering and pacing, but she said that is a problem in nursing homes and there really is not much they can do. We don't want to overmedicate, which would bring its own set of problems. It is better that she stays mobile.

May 31, 2013

The work has progressed furiously on Mom's life book this week. I had believed that the old photos of her and the family would trigger memories, but this is not the case. I have read that it is good to play music from the era that the dementia patient will remember the most, and that sometimes, they even sing along. Yesterday, I recalled Mom's favorite song was Al Di La, an Italian song from a movie out of the 60's. Back then, she bought the 45 rpm single and played it over and over and over again on the hi-fi. I found it on the computer and played it for her, but she had no recognition.

Back in 1997, I asked Mom and Dad to complete memory books to record all the important events, circumstances, and people in their lives. She was so lucid then; it was just sixteen years ago. As I was reading, I felt like I was getting to know her all over again. There were so many memories, a whole lifetime shuttered away in the recesses of her mind. I thought this new life book with the photos would help her to remember. I don't know what to do. I will continue to work on her life book. Maybe its purpose is to actually help me to remember all the good times in her life. This may help me face the challenge of caring for her now.

The challenge we face is not so much the feeding, toileting, cleaning, and dressing her. The greater challenge is the constant supervision and trying to redirect her frustration and impatience when she is not even aware herself why she paces and eats obsessively.

3

Family was everything. Mom and Dad loved their kids and grandkids. They were the very center of their lives. They attended every birthday party and holiday gathering, and mom would always bring the cake. She baked "money" cakes for the grandkids. This consisted of boiling nickels, dimes, and quarters and placing them in the cake batter before baking. She finished by assembling and frosting the cakes. Almost before those grandkids were passed their slices, little fingers would be diving into that cake with crumbs flying everywhere in search of that money, gloating excitedly over who found the most quarters. Ah, what a happy memory.

[Journal Entries]

June 2, 2013

The routine that I have tweaked is working pretty well. I have learned that my shower and feeding of the dog and cat needs to be done before I enter Mom's room to ready her for the day. I then make sure she toilets, wash her hands and face, dress her, and clean her teeth. She can still tie her shoes—yea! (It is peculiar which memories stick.) We then fix and eat breakfast. It is now time to do yoga until 9:00 a.m. when Joyce Meyer comes on television to teach us how to better know God. We try to take care of her physical *and* spiritual needs. Fulfilling emotional needs are more of a challenge. I turn on the television so she can watch "I Love Lucy" or "The Dick Van Dyke Show" and maybe the game shows "Let's Make a Deal" and "The Price is Right". But alas, very little can hold her attention these days due to having very little comprehension of what is actually occurring.

The day then consists of juggling housekeeping, cooking, etc., while at the same time trying to keep Mom occupied and satisfied. I give her little tasks of the things she can do, but I have to be creative to come up with those. We start out for a walk, but it is not long before she says her back hurts and we have to go back home. Sometimes time stands still, but then it races by. I can't help myself, so I show her photos or relate some tidbit of our past life to search her face for some depth of recognition. Sometimes she smiles and says, "Yes", but then she slips away again. I showed her the photo of her three daughters when I was one year old, and she finally said, "Yes, I know them."

I said, "Well, that little one is Ronnie, and that's me."

Surprised, she says, "Oh really? It doesn't look like you".

"I'm a lot older now".

"I am, too".

We both laughed.

Tonight, as she climbed into bed, I read aloud a chapter of a Nancy Drew mystery. She listens intently and always thanks me when I am done. I hope my words and actions show her that I love her, and she can absorb that in the recess of her heart, if not her mind.

June 5, 2013

This morning, Mom sat with me as I worked on her life book. I sorted the photos of her young granddaughters and asked if she knew who they were.

"Young girls," was her reply.

I said, "Yes, your granddaughters, Tiffy and Sissy".

She just shook her head. I then brought out her own wedding picture, and she didn't recognize herself or her groom. When I told her that she was married to Harold and asked if that brought back any memories, she said, "No, what's wrong with me, anyway?"

I took this controversial opportunity to tell her that she has a disease that steals away her memory. She said "Oh, I'm just no good." I assured her it was not her fault--and she is good-- it is just a disease. Trying to elicit her memories can have a down side when it causes frustration. However, I have seen seasoned caregivers resort to lying to memory care patients, telling them anything, just to get through a moment, with the logic that they won't remember it the next moment anyway. This seems cruel to me and strips away dignity. These patients deserve the respect of the truth. A topic may come up that we know would hurt them or further confuse them. In this situation, it may be better just to redirect the conversation to a safer topic, if possible.

June 18, 2013

This past week, our brother-in-law died unexpectedly. This event brought us out-of-town guests. Availability of our caregivers was at a minimum, so Mom was included in our very, very busy week. She was confused with people coming and going, but she did as well as she could. I can see she tries so hard to function appropriately. She endured long car rides quite well, although she made some inappropriately loud remarks at the funeral home such as, "Why are we here?" and "When do we leave?"

On the fourth day, she drove with us to the cemetery for interment, to a luncheon afterward, and then on to Jim's sister's home to visit awhile with the immediate family. I always make sure to fix her a plate of food, cut her meat, and get her settled before I get my own. She likes to follow me wherever I go. When I went to the bathroom, she got confused and asked Jim's niece if she could, "go upstairs to my room now?" It was quite a long day. We left our home at noon and did not return until 9:00 p.m. On the journey home, she kept repeating, "Are we going to my home now? Do I have a home? Can we get to my home?"

Today her "home" questions continue. She turned to me and asked, "Do you live close to here?" When I told her I lived here, she said she was really glad, because "You're nice". I learn to cherish the small things.

June 24, 2013

Today, Wendi, Chase, and I went strawberry picking, while Julie stayed with Mom. When we got home, we made jam. I thought it might be good to involve Mom, so I had her stir the strawberry and sugar mixture. A couple weak stirs later, she said, "I just can't do it anymore". Then I was hoping that she would be content to sit and visit with us in the kitchen while we worked, but mid-way through the canning process, she rose and began wandering, stopping only long enough to say, "Can I go upstairs to my room now?" and, "What am I supposed to do?" So, with some distractions, we managed to get the strawberry jam put up and Mom settled, and it really turned out to be a wonderful day.

June 30, 2013

I just received news that my cousin died last night. That is the second family death in two weeks. Another funeral to attend. Mom will not attend with me unless I cannot find a caregiver. She doesn't remember who I am or who our cousin was. Today she spoke of her brothers and how they "could do anything".

I said, "Do you remember how many brothers you had?"

She replied, "Four" (She had three). I asked if she recalled her brothers' names. She replied, "Ronnie" (but she never had a brother with my name). In her fitfulness today, she roamed into the kitchen and took two cookie doughs off the cookie sheet and wrapped them in a brochure for our upcoming Balloonfest. She strolled with them happily into her room, insisting on going to bed at 2:00 p.m. I cut up some apple and offered it to her, but she refused that while trying to hide the brochure filled with cookie dough. She is getting pretty good at sneaking food, especially sweets. She went to bed to take a nap, and about an hour later, she poked her head out of her room, and I noticed she had no dentures. That started our search for the dentures, which we finally found on the top of her dresser.

I struggle with frustration, which sometimes turns to humor, which then leads to guilt, because my humor over some of her actions feels like disrespect, especially when I justify the humor as a means to relieve my stress or maintain my sanity. However, laughter is good medicine and it just may be okay to laugh a little.

She can't help what she does—it is the disease. Every window in her brain is shut and locked. There is agitation and confusion in late-stage dementia because their brain recalls scattered fragments, bits and pieces of their lives, but there are so many missing pieces, the fragments have nothing to connect to, and nothing makes sense anymore. My most profound hurt is the constant reminder that where there is no memory of our relationship, there is no memory of love. Where did my mama go? The love between a mother and child is profound, but now I have to love her enough for both of us; but always with God, the author of love, leading the way.

4

Traveling played a large part in the lives of the Lee family. Daddy had the nomad spirit, but Mom went with him every time. He never went anywhere without her. The last family trip was a cruise to the Bahamas in 1997. This was Mom and Dad's third trip to the Bahamas, but they wanted to share it with their children and grandchildren—one more time. The last trip together.

[Journal entries]

July 14, 2013

We rented a cottage on Lake Huron, a couple hours away. Jim and I returned yesterday after a one-week reprieve (well-deserved I think). Leslie came up from Atlanta and stayed at our house to be Mom's caregiver. She did not relate any problems or details; however, she did say that I should hire the caregiver for an extra half-day mid-week to give me more time off, so Julie will now visit us three half-days a week. Why are we so happy when someone else walks a mile in our shoes? I don't feel so alone anymore. But now I must settle back into the routine.

Mom's mealtimes are more of a challenge to her now. While I cut her food into bite-size pieces, she still views it as too large and tries to cut it up with her fork even smaller, but is usually unsuccessful and just gives up saying she's "full". I give her apple pieces to eat, and today she ate those pieces but ate around the skins, despite being told five times that it was okay to eat the whole thing. We have to find foods that are easier for her to manage, like pancakes.

It is difficult for me today to return to our routine. Sometimes, I feel that the difficulty dealing with the grief of so much that is lost is worse than the physical caring for my mother. At times, my foreboding drags me down like a wind-driven raging storm. Today was one of those days. I had no energy to fight it and couldn't accomplish much. I unpacked a little. I took a nap when Mom took a nap. I hope I have more energy tomorrow.

July 21, 2013

Sometimes I wonder, why does God allow people to live long lives when their minds are gone? Yet in my relationship with God, it's fruitless to ask that question because as we learned at church today, "God's grace is sufficient for us, and in our weaknesses, He is made strong". He is walking with us through this valley, after all, and oh, the lessons I am learning along the way. With some resistance on my part, he is nevertheless teaching me patience, perseverance, love, commitment, respect, and the list goes on. These are exhausting lessons, but above all these, stands trust. Trusting in God who loves me and loves my mom and knows what is best. Trusting Him to do the right thing at the right time and to be with me in this valley of the shadow of her death brings me comfort and peace of heart that surpasses all of my understanding. Though the shadow is always nipping at our heels, God goes before us to lead the way.

July 30, 2013

Although disease continues to loot my mother's memories, I still love who she used to be and who she is now, very much indeed. What a good mother she was, and still is. She sewed all our clothes, sewed our choir robes for church, and then sewed our wedding dresses and bridesmaid dresses. She even crocheted a gorgeous wedding dress for my Barbie doll so many years ago. She could be relied on to always be there when we needed her; so much to be thankful for.

Then along the way, our relationship experienced some turbulence. When I was a teenager, my puberty striking simultaneously with her menopause was a recipe for disaster. I had a bad attitude, and she did not have the patience to deal with it. It didn't help that this occurred during the pandemonium that defined the 1960's. From that point forward, we rarely saw eye to eye on the finer points of life. But now, it's as if we've started on a new foot, given a new chance, a new dance. Trivial differences don't matter when the challenges are daily survival such as keeping her fed, calm, and safe. When we've managed to do that, it is a good day.

5

The following is an excerpt from Mom's memory book that she completed in 1997, in her own words:

"When I consider the future, I don't have much that I would like to do anymore. I just hope we can stay active and golf for many more of our years. Would like to keep our health fairly good and not become an invalid. Would, if possible, like to have a quality life until the end. Hope our family stays close and together as much as possible. We are always interested in the lives of our children, grandchildren and great-grandchildren. Hope they accomplish all the things they like in life."

[Journal entries]

August 6, 2013

Sometimes it is hard for me to write, struggling with this day-to-day caregiving and seeing her slip subtly away more each day. In her own words, she stated she wanted to have a quality of life to the end. None of us can know what the future holds. This disease not only steals memories, but it removes the ability to understand that your memories are being stolen away, causing the paranoia and inner struggle, and even anger, we see so much with this disease. For me, the wrestling match becomes whether or not I'm making any difference in her life. Just as I watch the flowers in my garden reach their peak and then the beautiful pedals begin to fall one-by-one, so my mother's memories fall, one-by-one. Six years ago, I took for granted when my mother would speak of my dad and say, "I still miss him", for now she doesn't recognize his photo, and has no memory of him at all. Today she recited one line of the "Lord's

Prayer" at church. One year ago, she could recite every line.

This afternoon, she consented to do aerobics with me, and then we took a walk up the road. Her moods will vary, but then, so do mine. Simply put, oftentimes her mood seems to improve when my mood improves. She seems much less anxious when I am kind and loving and upbeat. I like to see her laugh, so I do whatever I can to make her laugh. Watching funny animal clips on television makes her laugh. Laughter is good medicine. It is good to find what works and stick with it (until another change comes along).

August 10, 2013

The mind is a strange contraption. What an insidious disease that will not allow you to recognize the elementary necessities, like eating, and even toiletry. Mom needs help with all the basic functions when using the bathroom. She has urinary incontinency.

Each day can be a new adventure without even escaping the confines of our home. She no longer recognizes the meat or vegetables on her plate. I not only have to cut up her food, now I need to remind her which utensil to use or which foods are finger foods. She leaves her plate littered with food fragments, it would appear, because she simply doesn't know what they are. She sits back and says, "I am full". She was never picky with her food before. Curiously, she never turns down a cookie, piece of pie, cake, or ice cream. Her sweet tooth remains intact. How very puzzling.

August 11, 2013

For a distraction today, Mom, Jim, and I went to Frankenmuth, Michigan, a quaint old German tourist city. When she rode as a passenger with my dad driving, Mom always had a habit of telling him when the coast was clear, or if cars were coming when they stopped at an intersection. Now she rides in the passenger seat up front with Jim when we travel, and she tells him, "It's okay this way," or, "There's a car coming". She does this so automatically. How very odd, the things that stay glued in our minds, when other, more important things have slipped away. It is very sweet, really. Jim finds me in the rear-view mirror as I now sit in the back seat, and we smile our knowing smiles. We look forward to her traffic reports.

When we arrived at Frankenmuth, we took a paddle-boat ride, did some shopping, and ate a fabulous fried chicken dinner. Although she will not remember any of this tomorrow, we all enjoyed the day, for today is all we truly have, anyway. The past is forgotten, and tomorrows are not promised.

I am not quite sure where middle age ends and old age begins; it depends on one's perspective. I like to believe I'm in middle age. Since I retired, all the stress of that job has rolled off my shoulders, down my back, and made a mud puddle on the floor that I was able to sweep up and pitch out. It was a blessing to help and serve people in my job, but being a public servant in some capacity or another for more than thirty years brings a draining condition called burn-out. Since my retirement, I have not felt this alive since before my middle age began. The walls of cynicism and skepticism that I must have built over years of serving angry people are being peeled away like a thick-skinned orange to reveal the sensitive, placid disposition of the child I think I once knew I was, yet tempered with the hard-learned experiences that have brought me to a wiser plateau of content-edness. As I once heard in a movie, I have found my smile again. What a privilege to now be able to care for my mom. It is the best, hardest job I've ever had.

August 20, 2013

Oh, how I've come to savor my haven at day's end with my dog at my feet and my heating pad on my aches and pains. These days spent with Mom are surreal in a way. She tries to communicate, but a sentence usually comes out in a mish-mash of words, and I have no idea what she means. When she attempts at correcting herself, the second attempt is usually worse until she just waves her hand and says, "Oh, forget it". What does come across loud and clear, however, is her repeated questioning as to "Why am I here?" and "Where am I supposed to be now?" and "Where do I go?" or "When are they coming to get me?" (She is referring to the caregivers at the assisted living home who used to come to take her to a meal). Her mind is still operating in the routine of the assisted living home.

Not only does she have no memory of me now, she has no memory of Daddy or other family members. She doesn't even understand what the words "husband and daughter" mean. So much is lost. It seems we may take a step forward, only to take two steps back. Today was cleaning day, which means a challenging day because when I cannot spend time with her, she wanders. The emotions are draining out of me, and I need help. I am tested to my limits and found wanting. In the next couple weeks, I'm planning to walk to raise funds to end AD with the Alzheimer's Association. We can only hope someone will find a cure for this disease.

August 22, 2013

The days spent with Mom are becoming routine. Extraordinary circumstances are becoming ordinary occurrences. There are no new and unusual behaviors except for subtle downslides further and further away from us. She used to have occasional "good" days when she would recall some memory that would surprise us, or maybe she would function somewhat normally. I haven't seen any "good" days from her in what seems like a long, long time. Yet this day is no ordinary day.

Today we woke up to learn that our sister-in-law has a terminal cancer, unexpected and out of the blue. This is unbelievable. The briars are growing thicker in this valley we are struggling through. The heart rides on many roller coasters in life. When I was young, I loved passionately. Then as I grew, my love became bruised, trampled, and crushed by failed expectations, bad choices, physical challenges, loss, and disappointments, until I filed for emotional bankruptcy and became numb to the pain of loss. Somewhere along the line, my emotions flat-lined.

This was quite a while ago. Fortunately, now as I feel God's love for me, I can feel God's love for others. It is like God wants to love others *through* me.

This love is so strong today for my sister-in-law that I just had to reach out to her. Since they did not want any contact by phone, I wrote her a letter to offer encouragement and prayer in agreement for her healing. The death of the spirit is worse than the death of the body, and it is my desire to never tread those waters again, for there is no fulfillment in the state of a spiritual coma. True fulfillment comes with sharing love, for when all is said and done, love is all that truly matters, and is the only thing we can take with us when we leave this life behind; and it is the only thing of value that we leave behind.

August 25, 2013

To love a person with AD is truly a study in unconditional love. We have to wonder how it is possible that a sufferer of AD could hold a flicker of love for people they do not recognize or have any memory of, even if it is their own child. Is it the memories that create the bond that forms the love? For instance, I love my mother because of those memories created by the experiences we shared in our mother-daughter relationship, even subconscious memories of her nurturing me when I was a baby. I clung to those good moments as a child when she nurtured me with stability, security, and understanding borne of love and caring. Then I grew up and pursued my life.

Now, in the last twelve years, the roles have reversed, and the ravages of disease have rendered her increasingly more childlike. My daytime routine of caregiving does not leave much room for displays of affection, but maybe just by *doing* those caregiving tasks, I am nurturing her as she once nurtured me, and there is hope that maybe a love is rekindled deep in her spirit. Her spirit does not have Alzheimer's. I still say, "I love you" when I read her a story and tuck her into bed at night. Yet it is in the quiet still of the night when I think back over the day, that I wonder, did I show her enough times that I love her?

Because I do, even knowing the love may not be returned, or at least not *shown*. It is a good day when I can make her smile. I cling to her smiles now like a life preserver.

August 27, 2013

A storm raged outside our windows today, but it did not penetrate the walls of my house. All was peaceful within. Mom laughed today and was cooperative to my suggestions. She agreed to get out of her chair to do yoga. Oh, to be sure that her attempts at yoga do not resemble anything like yoga, but it is so good for her to move and stretch. When I tell her that she is doing great, she is encouraged and tries even harder. I am so proud of her when she tries because I know how much back pain she has. To top it off, today was also my cleaning day, which I normally dread because she becomes restless and anxious when I cannot give her my undivided attention, but today seemed different. A kind of peace settled down upon our routine today, and we enjoyed each other's company. It was a feeling as if she trusted me and was not anxious. This entry will be good to refer back to on future days that are more challenging. This day was our "one step forward".

6

It was in June of 1992, that Ruth and Harold celebrated their fiftieth anniversary party. It was a catered affair attended by family and friends on a pretty summer day. One of the attendees was Mom's sister Gladys, who was older than mom by fourteen years. At this time, Gladys suffered from Alzheimer's disease and was in the exact same stage that Mom would be in, about fourteen years later. There was a continuous video playing of the home movies Daddy took in the 1940's and 1950s; as well as Super 8 movies I took in the 1970's. I recited a little ditty I prepared especially for the occasion:

They met on a News hike,
Where she fell over his shoe,
Now fifty years have passed,
Since they said "I do" in '42.

They established a home,
With a collie named Bonnie,
Then in orderly fashion,
Came Leslie, Laurie, and Ronnie.

They were a family of five,
Who happily traveled and built a new house,
Several more years passed as they thrived,
'Til the girls each took a spouse.

The children had children,
With several years in between,
Six girls and two boys,
Brought the number to sixteen.

They united and gathered for special occasions,
Like birthdays and Christmas and Halloween;
The children's children had children,
Raising the total to nineteen.

So congratulations Ruth and Harold,
On a marriage fifty years old,
All those years of training,
Has earned you the Gold!

[Journal entries]
September 1, 2013

This morning brought a new wrinkle. The incontinency she's been experiencing at night has now extended into the daytime. After breakfast this morning, she stood in the kitchen and said her pants were "red" on this leg, but not the other leg.

I said, "No, they don't look red".

She said, "Yes, I don't know why, but it's this leg, and it's still there".

As I looked down, I could see a puddle forming on the floor and her shoe was wet. It took a couple seconds to register what was happening. As I changed her clothes, threw her shoes in the trash, and cleaned up the puddle, my heart was heavy with the anguish of what I was actually doing. Another mile marker goes by on the perilous journey called Alzheimer's.

She was very anxious this afternoon with the incessant pacing and usual refrains of "Where am I supposed to be?" and "I want to go to bed". I am learning not to argue with her and just let her do what she wants to do. When she goes into her bedroom, she either: lays in bed and calms down, or comes out again anyway because she really doesn't know what she wants to do. Sometimes it helps for me to make suggestions, like, "Why don't you do this, or do that?" On occasion, this method will help her and she can make a decision; other times, she cannot. I have learned that it is usually easier to go along with what she wants to do or else she becomes very agitated. It is a gentle balance that can go either way. Each moment is a new adventure with no guarantee of what the next moment will bring.

September 2, 2013

Today Jim and I hosted our neighborhood Labor Day party, with a flurry of cooking, cleaning, and preparation. I bought Mom new clothes and stood on the firm belief that she would relish the company and might savor being around the neighbors she has come to be familiar with. I was mistaken. She was very anxious today. Her habit of following me wherever I go proved to be very difficult while trying to host a party since I was in and out of the house many times while serving the picnic dinner. I resorted to asking a friend to sit with her for a few minutes so I could fix her a plate of food.

Fortunately, after dinner, Chase was working at the table with his building toys and Mom was most content when the three of us sat quietly at the table together. Thus, spending so much time with my mother inside, I missed a large part of the party outside, but all was good—I didn't mind. It was fun spending time building with my grandson and it was comforting to see mom content for a time. It was a challenging day and one I would not want to repeat anytime soon, however, the challenge was surmountable.

September 3, 2013

I am able to manage Mom's physical care, and we have a good routine in place. I took her for a ride to the grocery store and a visit to my old county office where we spent a good forty-five minutes visiting, but that was only good until we got home, when her agitation and pacing took over. I am not infallible.

Sometimes, when I hear, "When do I eat?" or "I want to go to bed" for the hundredth time, I want to scream, but I don't.

Today was like that. Maybe I need to scream. I could go upstairs, put my pillow over my face, and scream as loud as I can. The "Serenity Prayer" helped me. "God grant me the serenity to accept the things I cannot change, the courage to change the things I can, and the wisdom to know the difference". I picked up one of my crossword puzzles, which always relieves my mind of stress, but her barrage of questions and anxiety seem to intensify when I am not giving her my undivided attention. I just do not know how much longer I can do this.

September 6, 2013

While traveling home from the grocery store today, with Mom in the passenger seat, listening to my favorite 1960's oldies music wafting from the radio, I experienced déjà vu'. I went back in time to age sixteen. I just got my driver's license, and I was driving our white three-speed 1966 Mustang with ivy-gold bucket seats. I looked over and pictured Mom as I once knew her (when she was the mom and I was the teenager). At any moment, I would hear her expected refrain, "Do they call that music?" I relished being in that moment and happily lingered there for a while.

My mom has always been brave. Two years earlier, when I was fourteen-years-old, in July of 1967, Detroit was burning. President Johnson called in five thousand federal troops to help quell the riots. There were a lot of angry people out there, as the unrest grew around the country. My grandmother needed rescuing before the fires reached her home, so I rode with my mom from our home in the suburbs to Grandma's house in Detroit, the first house off of Grand River Ave. near Greenfield. I have a vivid memory of traveling our familiar route down Grand River Avenue into Detroit, but there was nothing familiar about the scene before me now. Black smoke filled the horizon, and there were federal troops wearing camouflage and helmets, cradling their M-16's, lined up on both sides of the road. It was a surreal experience and one I certainly never expected to see in my own hometown.

It was back to reality after arriving home, and I prepared to send e-mails to my sisters regarding a decision on whether or not to obtain a "Do Not Resuscitate" (DNR) order. This order alerts EMS, hospitals, and doctors to not resuscitate the patient, should there be a life-threatening occurrence. There is much thought that must go into such a decision, to include quality of life, and the sometimes-violent methods that must be used to resuscitate (which could result in broken ribs), as well as to consider all Mom's medical conditions. Mom is not ready for hospice/end-of-life care, and I don't expect a disaster to occur. It is just that when you have a ninety-one-year-old sleeping under your roof, it would be prudent to be prepared for all emergencies.

Mom has cardiovascular issues. Each and every morning when I wake up, I dread going into her room, not knowing what I might find there. As I open the blinds, I say, "Time to rise and shine," and hold my breath until she answers me. The medical power of attorney Mom completed all those years ago, has greatly aided us in making this decision. We know that it was her decision herself not to be kept alive by artificial means. This is just one more necessary piece of paper. I would get the DNR order completed as soon as possible.

She ate a good dinner tonight, despite pulling all the toppings off her pizza and scooting them into a pile on her plate. There have been no games or coloring in quite a while. Do I really want further evidence of her decline? The games were not teaching her anything, except frustration. My new motto: if it helps, do it; if it doesn't help, don't do it. As the months go by, I've come to realize it is not so important to force her into the box of structure that I thought was necessary for her to thrive. She was not thriving. Now, if she wants to go to bed, I let her. If she doesn't want to eat her dinner, it gets tossed out. If she wants to eat cake, I let her. This is perhaps my most difficult challenge—to respect her wishes, even if it may not be in her best interest.

She is ninety–one–years-old after all; she has earned the right to make her own choices, so long as I can prevent her from mass self-destruction. It is a delicate balance. After tucking her into bed tonight, she said to me, "Thank you for coming".

September 8, 2013

Today is sunny and warm, more like a mid-summer's day. It is a beautiful day to walk for Alzheimer's. After raising money for our cause, Jeff, Wendi, Chase, and I set out to Brighton for our Walk to End Alzheimer's Disease, organized by the Alzheimer's Association. We bought purple shirts that read, "I Walk for Alzheimer's". Most of the hundreds of people there did not actually have AD; they were just the caregivers and relatives who were affected by it. The amount of people this disease affects is staggering. Sooner or later, almost no one is left unscathed. Long-stemmed pinwheel flowers in different colors were distributed; the colors represented whether you had AD, whether you were a relative or caregiver of someone with AD, or whether you lost someone to AD. We carried a yellow flower signifying we were the caregivers of someone with AD. A lump rose in my throat when I wrote "Ruth Lee" across the petals, a public admission that she is actually a victim of this horrible malady.

There were rows of booths containing sponsors distributing brochures and other paraphernalia, and we loaded up our bag. The sponsors were various organizations such as assisted living homes, adult foster-care homes, medical colleges, governmental agencies, caregiver agencies, hospital agencies, and all sorts of associations offering services to assist AD patients and their caregivers. The organizers soon stepped up to the podium and offered startling statistics, as well as the goals for fundraising, giving us pep talks and thanking us for our efforts. It was almost a festive mood. There was even a marching band to spur us on our way.

We had the choice of hiking a three-mile walk or a one-and-a-half-mile walk. With a five-year-old in tow, we believed it was wiser to opt for the one-and-a-half-mile walk, and so we set out.

The walk took us down some back streets and then back along the busy main street of town, and Chase soon grew tired, as we expected he would. But as we walked with a new resolve, we proudly raised up our pinwheel flower like it was a banner and we were marching off to war in a battle to fight to save our loved one back home. It was a poignant time of reflection for me.

Last week, I began having wild dreams that someone found a cure for AD and all the so-called "tao tangles" fell off all those affected brains. Then suddenly, all the doors at every nursing home, adult foster-care home, assisted living home, and memory-care facility were flung wide open and hordes of people walked out into the light of the sun with decades of their stolen memories fully restored. Stolen loot recovered. What a glorious day that would be, indeed!

September 12, 2013

We just finished our living room aerobics. Exercise is a balm for the spirit. Mom's severe arthritis in her back limits her stamina, so her moves don't resemble the ones on the video, but she is up and moving and stretching and, best of all, smiling. I love the smiling.

Yesterday morning, I had an altercation with a family member. I was left standing in the kitchen with pumping adrenaline and despair to the point of dropping my head in my hands and sobbing. I couldn't stop the tears. Mom wandered into the kitchen, and my heart ached to have her come over to me and put her arms around me and tell me everything would be okay. But with a perplexed look on her face, she just turned and walked into the other room. She simply just didn't understand. But it was in that very instant that Jesus put his arms around me and reminded me that He would never leave me nor forsake me, and what a glorious demonstration of His love that was.

In the early afternoon, I learned that my 6:00 p.m. golf date with the girls was moved up to 4:00 p.m. It is amazing what challenges a two-hour change can present to a caregiver, listed as follows:

1) Jim would not be home from work to watch Mom until 4:45 p.m.

2) The afternoons are Mom's more restless times, when she continuously says she wants to go to bed. When Mom goes to bed without my assistance, she knows she has to change into her pajamas, although she doesn't quite know what those are, so she undresses and takes clothes out of her closet, and strews them around her room, not remembering what she needed to do.

3) It is too early to administer the evening medications, which include a pain pill and a sleeping pill.

4) I will need to make an early dinner so she doesn't get hungry and begin grazing.

However, even taking all this into consideration, we are overcomers! I made dinner at 3:00 p.m., dressed Mom in her pajamas, asked our neighbor, Bob, to sit with her until Jim got home an hour later, and I hoped for the best. While I was driving off the first tee, I suddenly had a terrifying vision of Mom undressing and totally surprising Bob into an embarrassed conundrum. I was relieved when I arrived home before sunset and found that even though Mom had been restless, her pajamas were safely intact. I gave her the medications, read her a story, and tucked her into bed. All's well that ends well. The key to caregiving is to plan ahead when you can.

September 19, 2013

It was a calmer day today than we had yesterday. We went shopping for new shoes for Mom. We narrowed it down to two pairs. As she took off one pair, I told her to try on the other pair, and then I asked her to try on the first pair again and to tell me which pair felt better. That is where I made my mistake. She then proceeded to take on and off those two pairs of shoes, not really understanding that we were looking for how they fit. In fact, after the fourth switch, she then grabbed her old shoe and said, "What about this one?"

I realized she was unable to comprehend why she was trying on the shoes, and it was time for me to pick a pair, because she could not. I had to press down on her toe, to see how much room she had at the end of the shoe (reminiscent of how I had to buy baby shoes for my kids). I hope I made the right choice.

September 24, 2013

I have fallen into bed utterly exhausted tonight. A hubbub of household chores and waiting on Mom has left me spent. I was utterly distracted by activity this afternoon when I noticed Mom coming out of the laundry room, pulling up her pants, saying she had to go potty. To my horror, I discovered she had urinated on top of the kitty litter box. Another cleaning job added to the list. At dinnertime lately, when she doesn't want to eat her meal, she says, "I'm full". That is, until I offer her dessert, then she is suddenly not full. Tonight, when I was getting her ready for bed, she said, "I love you".

When I told her I loved her too, she said, "I really do love you". Her heart says what her brain can't. Wow, that was totally unexpected, but very, very needed and welcomed. The good makes the bad worthwhile, and that is what I will choose to dwell on as I drift off into my much-needed slumber.

7

In 1990, Mom and Daddy found a cat sitting outside the sliding door of their condo, looking mournfully in at them. They have always been a soft touch where animals are concerned, so they started to leave food for it outside. One day, it never came back, and they missed that little guy, so off they went to the animal shelter, where they found and adopted a big tiger tom-cat named Jack. He was no longer a kitten, but no one could tell his age for certain. Jack became their treasured companion. They bought cat toys, and Daddy's new hobby became building carpeted play towers and fashioning more toys for Jack to play with. Jack witnessed many changes in their lives.

The sad day he realized Daddy was not coming back, Jack grew closer to Mom and would snuggle with her, sit on her lap, and sleep in her bed. Mom brought him to the assisted living home in 2009. Thirty days after Mom moved in with me in 2013, Jack died. He was twenty-three-plus-years old. Such an advanced age lends itself to distinction. Jack was with Mom through difficult times and he deserves an honorable mention here.

[Journal entries]
October 6, 2013

It's been a week and a half since I've written. I underwent left shoulder surgery on September 25, and my days are filled with one-handed challenges and battling pain. Of course, Mom, not knowing any different, needs the same care she is accustomed to, despite my hindrances. I thank God for my caregivers, Julie and Jeanne, and a good schedule so Mom does not lack for anything. But I should not fail to mention my most attentive caregiver, Jim, who has tended to my every need, and I'm so grateful for him. I've had many surgeries on my joints, and I hope this is my 1st one. Somehow God is working all this out.

Yesterday, Mom asked me if I lived far from here. I told her I lived here, this is our home, and she lives with us. She said, "Oh, I didn't know that. No one told me." Five minutes later, Mom said, "Do you live far from here?"

October 9, 2013

I've been reading a book called, *Change Your Words Change Your Life* by Joyce Meyer. Therefore, I'm trying to rid my heart of damaging and negative thoughts because where the thoughts are, the words are not far behind.

I know that when a person is faced with a loved one who has memory loss and requires monumental care, there is a tendency to want to place them in a home, certainly some safe environment where they will be cared for, yet causing, sadly, the least interruption to their own lives. I had seen this many times in my career at the Veteran's office. This certainly seemed to be an easier solution when I was faced with the choice. For many people, their choices are limited, due to careers, limited living space, or other obligations. In truth, for all of us, it is very painful to watch your loved one decline to an inevitable morbid outcome. No one wants to be the one that has to watch that happen. Oh, how we prefer to remember them as they were, and not witness the steady decline and what the disease will render them in the end. Human nature causes us to self-preserve—we tend to turn away from situations that offer no hope. Yet, there is still much to be thankful for. Just her presence to me is a blessing. She may have lost her memories, but she is still the same person. She is still my mom, and I will have no regrets.

October 12, 2013

Every morning when I enter Mom's room, I try to be upbeat, so first I say, "Time to rise and shine", and then as I open the window blinds, I sing "You are my sunshine, my only sunshine, you make me happy, when skies are gray. You never know, dear, how much I love you, please don't take my sunshine away". This is a good start to the day for both of us.

After breakfast, Mom and I went for a walk this morning. We must be quite a picture-- Mom hunched over her walker barreling down the street with me holding onto her, my arm in a sling, and walking my aged, overweight Maltese, Nellie, with my other hand. Mom has been walking farther this past week without mentioning her back hurting. Yesterday, I took her to the hairdresser, and she told the hairdresser my name was Leslie (my sister's name). Well, I was in the waiting room reading a book when the hairdresser called out "Leslie" two times before I finally realized she was trying to get my attention.

Last week, I was reminding Mom who Daddy was, saying they had been married for fifty-nine years, and when I asked if she recalled his name, she said, "Leslie". Leslie must be on her mind. This afternoon, Jim and I went to the show and to dinner for our "date night". Mom was still up when I got home since she wouldn't go to bed for Jeanne. Apparently, she was unsettled that I wasn't home. Although she doesn't remember my name, she seems to know I am the one constant in her life right now, and when I gave her a hug goodnight tonight, she held onto me really hard. We said our mutual "I love yous," and the forceful conviction of her words makes me to believe she really means it—words from her heart. What a joy to be able to experience her spirit speaking to me. I'd rather have her spirit words than brain words. If she was tucked away in a facility somewhere, we would not be able to share that, and what a loss 'that would be. I have been granted the grace not to lament over what is lost but to appreciate these small moments so much more.

October 23, 2013

Together, Mom and I watch our Bible-teaching show on television in the mornings. Mom does not act as if she is taking in the teaching, but I prefer to believe that her spirit is absorbing the words and that the Holy Spirit is revealing the meaning of those words to her heart and spirit.

This afternoon, Mom was able to articulate a question to me so I could grasp what she wanted to know. In her mind, she is still in her assisted living facility, even though she moved in with me six months ago. She wonders why the caregivers don't come to take her down to the dining room. Her world is a chaos of not understanding where she lives, why she doesn't remember anything, and the loss of who she was. But today, I saw in her eyes the desperate yearning to understand. I explained to her that she lives with me now and I'm her daughter and that when she was in her apartment at the other place, she was alone much of the time. Now one of us is with her all the time. Isn't that better?

She nodded, yes. I am learning, though, that sometimes her words of intent actually come out as something else. She'll say, "I want to go to bed" or, "I want to go to my room now," when she really just wants to go to the bathroom. I feel like I've been somewhat dense not to realize up until now that she could be saying one thing, but meaning another. I will try to be more astute to her needs. She still likes to laugh. A good goal to have: laugh more.

8

During their retirement years, the Lees were snowbirds. They would spend around six weeks in Florida during the winter so they could continue golfing and be outside, but when I found a job in Florida and made the move in 1985, they soon sold their condo and followed me south. I think they were disoriented when they were not around family. They figured they had two daughters down south, so down south is where they should be. Of course, to hear them talk, this was a move they have always wanted to try. I must say, I was content to know they were nearby. When I moved back to Michigan in 1987, their condo went up for sale and they moved back to Michigan one year later.

[Journal entries]
November 3, 2013

Laurie came to visit Mom yesterday. This was the first time Mom has seen Laurie since moving-in day. Was there recognition? Mom was animated when she greeted her. My sister held onto Mom's hand like she was afraid to let it go. As Laurie paged through Mom's life book, I heard her ask Mom the same questions I asked when we were putting the book together. Mom's responses are just non-committal nods of the head, or safe, generic answers. Laurie came to the sad realization that I had; there are just no memories of our family left at all.

Today I took Mom to breakfast, to the grocery store, to church, and for a ride in the afternoon. She had an insatiable appetite today. Four cookies, grapes, cashews, animal crackers, and a bread stick later, she was starting to get mad because she wanted dinner, and she wanted it now, reminding me every five minutes. Suffice it to say, I think I need more help than Mom does at this point. My patience resembles a stretched-thin rubber band. God, let your peace rain down on me and bathe me in the light and warmth of your love.

November 4, 2013

A battle is raging, but the battle is inside me. Mom's appetite and demands for food continues today. Despite three cookies, animal crackers, grapes, a Kit Kat, and cashews, she started in again with, "When am I going to get something to eat?"

I told her dinner would be ready in thirty minutes when Jim gets home from work. She responded, "I'm going to bed then".

I said "Okay", and she went to her bedroom and came out two minutes later. What is the solution to this?

November 15, 2013

It is finally Friday, but we primary caregivers work 24/7, so weekdays and weekends are all pretty much the same. It has been a rough week, with tense moments. I am not writing my memoirs to gloss over the rough spots and say how wonderful we're doing, or that I have all the answers, because I do not. We learn as we go. True, there are some ways to make a caregiver's life a little easier, but for the most part, it is day by day, moment by moment, and you never know what to expect next. Journaling does help to give perspective and to problem solve, but sometimes you just have to muddle through. It may be a good time to call a caregiver and just get away, even for a short period of time, to clear your head.

All week long, Mom was anxious and wanting food and never, ever, happy, arguing with me about every word that came out of my mouth. After eating numerous snacks again, she was peering over my shoulder as I was making dinner and getting angry because dinner wasn't done fast enough for her, so she just said, "I'm going to bed then".

I would say "Okay", and she would go to her bedroom, only

to come out again five minutes later asking the same questions. On one occasion when she did not come back out, I went to check on her, and she had taken off her slacks, grabbed a T-shirt, and had put her legs in the sleeves and pulled it up like pants, but then she couldn't understand why they wouldn't stay up.

Tonight, I was so anxious, I was at the breaking point. It was all I could do to get Mom ready for bed. I could not read to her as I normally would. God says that he is made strong in our weakness, so I am trusting He will show up to help me in my weakness, because He led me into this challenge, and I obeyed, so I have to believe He will equip me to do the job. Just as I am thinking these thoughts, Mom had a lucid moment. I believe that just for a little while, God, in His grace, brought her back to me. I hugged her and told her that I loved her.

She replied, "I love you more than you know". Wow.

Thank you, God, for giving my mom back to me tonight, even if only for a brief moment.

November 20, 2013

Three o'clock in the afternoon is the worst of times. This is when Mom's anxiety kicks into high gear. The barrage continues with "Can I get something to eat?" and then to, "I might as well go to bed now". Even while she was with me in the kitchen, watching me juggle pots and pans preparing dinner, she said, "I'm going to bed then".

I said, "Why don't you sit at the table; dinner will be ready in five minutes".

She sat for two minutes and then said, "I'm going to bed". Her memory span is much shorter than two minutes. After dinner, while I was doing dishes, she says, "Do you have far to go home?"

I said, "I am home and you live here, too".

Then she said something she never said before. She peered at me intently and said, "I think I knew you when we were young together". It seems she had some small window of memory from the past that emerged through the fog that has now become her brain. I saw this as an opportunity to delve a little further, so I asked if she remembered her sisters, Gladys and Sis. Without hesitation, she said, "Oh yes, I haven't seen them in a while, though". Then we had some good chuckles after dinner. Her mood seemed to improve after we ate. She became almost light-hearted.

November 21, 2013

It was a day spent at home because it was cold and dreary outside. Mom had severe back pain about 3:00 p.m., so she went to her room to lie down. I got her up for dinner, and she was better. After dinner I got quite a surprise. I gave her some medications, one pill at a time, with sips of water in between. When she was finished, I had her drink another good half-glass of water to wash them down. She then wanted to go to bed, so to get ready, we visited the bathroom. She walked over to the toilet, lifted the lid, and leaning over it, seemed to peer inside. Before I realized what was happening, she spit four of her pills into the toilet! I had no clue she had hidden the pills in her mouth; she was even talking to me in a normal fashion with them hidden in her mouth. She had never done anything like that before. It's time to come up with a new strategy. We're going to need to watch her like a hawk during medication distribution. She is also pretty good at getting into the food the minute I am out of sight. The way she sneaks food, you would think she never eats, but I feed her all day long!

November 29, 2013

We took Mom out to a buffet at a resort beautifully decorated for Christmas with our neighbors for Thanksgiving dinner. She enjoys venturing out of the house and being around people. She maintains proper etiquette while out in public, though it doesn't matter to me, I would take her out anyway, knowing she enjoys it so much.

Her bowels now are sluggish and not moving properly, so we have to find a balance between the right foods, water, juices, and stool softeners. Getting her to eat has also become more of a problem. Although she snacks between meals, at mealtimes now, she just stops eating. She doesn't want to eat what she doesn't recognize, and she doesn't recognize much of anything.

I can say, "You can eat that, it's your fruit," or, "That's your meat", but I may as well be speaking Chinese, because she doesn't know what that means. It is more often now that I have to place the food on her fork and hand it over to her to eat. She picks at her food, spreading it around her plate, but then wanders into the kitchen between meals looking for something to eat. Every day is truly a new adventure, but one that leaves me grappling with emotions. The wide spectrum of emotions include anguish, dread, anxiety, relief, regret, sorrow, guilt, fear, sadness, loss, just to name a slew, and each day I probably experience each of them many times over.

9

At the age of sixty, Mom passed the test for and was granted her real estate broker's license. She sold condos in the sales office of the condominium complex where they lived.

An excerpt from Mom's memory book:

"My advice to all future generations of our family would be to work hard at your profession. Get as much education as you can. Live a clean life and 'do unto others as you would have them do unto you'".

[Journal entries]
December 5, 2013

I've been debating tonight whether to write or not. The truth is, this disease is just not very pretty. There is nothing pretty about it. I try to "pretty it up" as I contemplate what Mom can still do. She can still walk short distances... I'm still thinking. What more can I come up with? The "pretty" list is pretty short. The ugly list of this disease is getting longer. I gave the list to her doctor this week, and her response was, "The next step is to think about hospice".

I asked Laurie for her advice on hospice because she is employed by an assisted living home and is more familiar with hospice. She extolled the benefits and services and all that they normally provide. I told Laurie I did not know what the end looked like for this disease; I didn't know what to expect. She only replied, "It's not pretty".

Then I spoke to my son, Roger, who worked as a certified nursing assistant. When I told him that mom continually says she wants to go home, or she wants to go to bed, he said, "She sounds depressed". For some reason, that never occurred to me before, but I can see that is true. It would be depressing to constantly be in a state of utter and total confusion. Hospice is normally for someone with a terminal illness with a prognosis of six months or less to live. It just doesn't seem practical to me to speak of calling hospice at this time.

Today when Mom told me she wanted to go home, I asked where "home" is, and she said, "Where my family is". I try to reason with her that I am her daughter, so I am her family, but the only family she talks of these days are her brothers. I am struggling with my own emotions. I want to make her happy, but I don't know how. Then I struggle around and around with what I call the full circle of emotions. One emotion leads to the next:
Love
Sadness (at all she's lost)
Frustration
Guilt (for being resentful)
Anger (at the disease)
Resentment (at overwhelming caregiving)
Desire (to make her life better)
Then they come around again, full circle.

Tonight, I wanted to show her that I love her so I gave her a long hug. As I held her, she said, "I just don't know what I'm supposed to do anymore". I said, "I know, I know, it's going to be okay." I know it is far better not to live by our emotions. Just keep doing what is right.

December 22, 2013

The last few weeks have flown by, preparing for Christmas and all that comes with it. Today, Jeff, Wendi, and Chase came over, and we made a holiday memory, baking Christmas cookies and assembling a gingerbread train. Their home lost power during the ice storm last night, so they were happy to be at our house, and were welcomed to stay over for a ham dinner. It was a festive and fun day for most of us, but sad to say, Mom did not have a good day. About noon, she commented that she was having pain going down into her thighs, as well as the pain continuing in her lower back. At times, her pain becomes so severe that her body actually begins to tremble, like she is in shock. The doctor did not want to increase the prescription pain medication she takes regularly, so I gave her an over-the-counter medicine that the doctor recommended.

Mom then went into her bedroom, but she did not lie down; she was up and pacing and restless. Wendi tried to include Mom in decorating the cookies, so she gave Mom a container of sugar sprinkles to shake onto the cookies, but Mom kept trying to squeeze the bottle with both hands, unable to grasp the concept of just shaking the sprinkles out, like you would a salt shaker. We had to abandon that idea. Mom then spent a little time in the chair watching us, but she soon became fidgety. At dinner, she tried to cut her bread with her fork and put her potatoes in her salad bowl, so I helped her to eat. After dinner, her anxiety became much worse as we were trying to clean up the kitchen and she wanted to go to bed, so I helped her do that.

Last night, Jim and I took Mom out to dinner. As we were driving home down our familiar neighborhood street, out of the blue she says, "I hope my daughter recognizes me. I haven't seen her in such a very long time". Where on earth, did that come from? The only explanation may be that we spoke to Leslie in Atlanta on the telephone the day before to wish her a happy birthday, so maybe, by some miracle, she connected that conversation with thinking she was on her way to visit her now? It was a clear, precise, and long sentence for her. Most of the time when she tries to speak, all the wrong words come tumbling out. I search for opportunities to hold a meaningful conversation so I could ease the pain of her confusion for just a little while.

December 25, 2013

It is wonderful to be able to spend Christmas Day with Mom, as I have had every Christmas Day during my lifetime. The day is now waning into the twilight hours. Last night (Christmas Eve) in church, Mom miraculously sang select phrases to "Silent Night", which she must have recalled from her childhood. This morning, she required maximum assistance to open her presents and really had no clue as to what anything was

Today, we visited Jeff, Wendi, and Chase's home, where we ate Christmas dinner and visited with family. During most of our visit, she repeated her mantra of telling everyone that she wanted to go home, wanted to go to her room, wanted to go to bed. I thought she may have been overstimulated by all the people, so I led her to the guest room to lie down, away from the noise. This did not seem to help. We had to leave early.

I had a horrifying thought. Her actions today were exactly what you would expect from a toddler. Could her mind really be reduced to that point? Sometimes it seems to me that my struggle is not with the disease so much as it lies within my own shortcomings. It is a test like no other, yet I can't help but feel that I'm missing something—the greater purpose why Mom is still this side of Heaven--and I don't know what I'm supposed to do to help her. I'm looking for a revelation on this one.

10

An excerpt from Mom's memory book:

"If I could have another trip, I'd like the boat trip to Alaska. We've already toured Europe four times. Been to Jamaica, Spain and Hawaii. Also been on Caribbean cruises and another one this year, March 1997. We've driven a good part of the U.S.A. also. There isn't much more to do. I just remembered I would like to see Greece & the Holy Land. Getting too old to travel that much now."

Mom did not make it to Alaska, Greece, or the Holy Land, but in April 2007, Leslie and I flew Mom to Myrtle Beach, South Carolina. We played miniature golf (she beat me), huddled together on the cold, windy beach wrapped up in blankets, toured the aquarium, and attended a dinner show, entertained and wooed by a Dean Martin impersonator. It was the last trip she was able to take, but it was a joyful one.

[Journal entries]

January 3, 2014

The New Year has crept up on us. The hectic pace slows after the holidays, and we settle in for the long winter stretch. The weather has been particularly bad this year—snow upon blowing snow, with temperatures at minus ten degrees this morning. This makes it nearly impossible to venture outside with a ninety-one-year-old. An extra pain pill has noticeably eased her pain, though the anxiety continues in the afternoons, especially nearing dinnertime. There is no rest for anyone until she gets dinner in her tummy. I have come to a reckoning that I need to work on my attitude, my responses, and my reactions, so that they come from a gentle, loving place in my heart, not only to ease Mom's anxiety, but to ease mine as well. The funny thing is, that loving place is also where peace lives, so when you have one, you also have the other; love and peace—two for the cost of one. They are often mentioned in the Bible together, and now I know why; you can't have one without the other. You can strive for one, but the other one comes as a bonus.

January 7, 2014

Last night, I was having a nightmare, and I wasn't even asleep! Mom's motion detector alarm woke me up every half hour, as she opened her bedroom door. Each time, I had to get up and put her back to bed. Somewhere towards the wee hours of the morning, with a pounding headache, I finally fell into an exhausted state of hibernation. This morning, I found her bed comforter on the living room sofa, her blanket bunched up on the living room chair, and when I went to her room, the door was open, and she was lying on her mattress with the mattress pad, the fitted sheet, and the flat sheet all lying on top of her. The pillow under her head was the toss pillow from the living room sofa. Everything else was helter-skelter. Some things made their way from the kitchen to her bedroom, including a partially eaten loaf of bread. The "sundown syndrome" has officially begun.

Today was a bitter cold day (-13°F) and the nightmare continued. She was very anxious and disoriented and kept speaking unintelligible words and asking for food. Most interestingly, at dinner and at bedtime, she spoke about her brothers and her sisters, repeatedly asking if she could go home. As I was tucking her into bed, she looked at me and said, "Where are my mom and dad?" I told her that her dad went to heaven when he was younger than me, and that her mother went to heaven when she was eighty-nine-years old in 1982. She said "That hurts". Maybe this was one of those times I should have changed the subject rather than telling her the truth. In her mind, she truly is in her childhood, missing her mom and dad. Since she was remembering her mom and dad, I suppose I wanted to foster that memory by telling her they were now in heaven, maybe to administer a dose of reality. I thought I could glean a flicker of awareness. It was not my intention to hurt her, but that is exactly what happened. If she asks me again, I will have to arrive at a more appropriate answer. Maybe I'll tell her that she will see them soon?

Tonight, Jim said that sometimes when a person is close to dying, they talk about their loved ones that have gone before. In my job in the Veterans office, I had similar conversations with others who have told me "death bed" stories of their loved one seeing deceased family members standing at their bedside, or even holding conversations with them. These are unexplained occurrences, something like being halfway between this world and the next world, and seem to vary with the individual. But then I reminded Jim that although Mom has exhibited quite a decline in the past year, she's really just beginning the "sundowning" stage and it is my understanding sometimes that can go on for a while. However, this disease can progress differently for different people, depending on the person's physical health, their age, and type of Alzheimer's (early onset or not), etc. I really don't know what to expect. It can also take a sudden turn. I am learning as I go.

Mom has been taking her memory medication for twelve years now, and the doctor says that at this stage in the disease, it is probably not serving its purpose to slow the progression of the disease any longer, so it was time to cut back. This medication is very expensive, so a couple weeks ago, we cut her back from two pills per day to one per day. Her increased erratic behavior may not be related to the reduced medication, but then who knows? Even the doctors say it is all experimental—yet to be proven. Her volatile behavior seems coincidentally connected to the reduced memory medication; therefore, starting today, we have returned her to the two pills per day. Every day of this journey is an experiment for me, what works and what doesn't.

January 8, 2014

A new day has dawned that was unlike yesterday's chaos. When Julie arrived this morning, we discussed Mom's increased erratic behavior. She told me that when her father suffered from AD, the gerontologist advised them not to reduce any memory medications because although they may not be beneficial for memory retention in the late stages, reducing the dose could adversely affect their behavior. This is something called "discontinuation syndrome". Bingo! Now it is all beginning to make sense—her erratic behavior, the sleepless nights, the mumbling, etc. To confirm our suspicions, last night I reinstated Mom's evening dose of the medication and she slept through the night, and we both had a happy, well-adjusted day today. I refilled her prescription today and feel very blessed that Mom had good insurance coverage because her co-pay was $112, but the insurer's share was over $900. That amounts to a total of more than $1,000 for three month's supply! That is the full amount we have to pay out-of-pocket at the end of the year when we have reached the limit that Medicare will pay.

Common sense is vital when caring for an AD patient. Every patient is different, and the solution that works for one patient, may not work for another, even if the circumstances seem the same. So many factors have to be considered like personality, character, memory level, relationship, and environment, to name a few. To be a good caregiver, I must be her advocate on her behalf to do what is best for her.

January 21, 2014

We are in the throes of winter, and bleak is the tone of my mood. I came to an impasse today. I have been trying so hard to make sure Mom has nutritious meals, exercise, and proper medication and hygiene. Taking care of these needs made me feel like I was doing my job. However, gradually she has not been eating her meals; she just lays her fork down and sits there. She argues about the exercise or refuses to do it, even when I try to make it fun for her. Yet she continues to hunt down and sneak cake and cookies, or even bread when I'm not looking. She seems to know just how to push my buttons.

I went through today devoid of feeling. My thoughts were this: at her age, if she doesn't want to eat her meals, I'm not going to force her. I'm not even going to ask her to exercise anymore. I hit bottom today. And here comes the circle of feelings--resentment, guilt, etc. One thing I learned today is that my working so hard for what I think she needs is not working at all. What I need to figure out now is how to let go. Trying to coerce her to do what I think is good for her, if she doesn't want to do it, is really not good for her at all because it causes strife, and strife is not good for either one of us.

It may sound petty, but rarely am I able to watch a television show that I want to watch without her getting huffy. My whole life revolves around her needs and her wants. I am searching today for balance. I feel I need to let go and let her be, do, and eat what she wants. Shouldn't a ninety-one-year old be allowed that right? But in reality, she isn't mentally ninety-one; she is only a toddler, and I am responsible for her care. That is my tug-of-war. I need to find the balance to keep her safe and thriving as much as possible, maintaining her dignity. Oh, if I could only have some peace of mind about this. I am being tossed by the storm, but I know Jesus can calm the storm, and I will, once again, find myself ashore on the other side.

January 22, 2014

Typically, I have not been writing every day, but yesterday was such a struggle, then the sun went down, the world turned, the sun came back up, and it is a new day. Some resolve and contentment came with this new day. I am working out the issues of the food and menu options. I know her eating habits are likely to only get worse, so I have resolved to buy canned protein drinks, protein bars, and other nutritious foods to supplement her diet. Someone suggested I should make her one large hot meal for lunch and a sandwich for dinner, but this would totally disrupt my household. The hours I spend now in meal-making would escalate if I had to make separate meals for everyone, and I fear my frustration would escalate as well. This does not seem like a solution, but a potential disaster. The healthy snacks would be a better solution. Advice is a good thing, and it is welcomed, but I have learned that when it comes to advice, absorb the good and discard what won't work for you. End of conversation.

January 26, 2014

This polar January has broken all records for frigid temperatures and snowfall since record-keeping began in Michigan. You have to think long and hard each day whether it's safe to venture outside with a tottery woman in her ninth decade. So, as you could well imagine, we just do not go out very much. Cabin fever sets in. Regardless, it was a good day.

While watching a woman's golf tournament on television, I said, "You used to play golf, didn't you?"

She said, "Yes, I did".

"You used to play with your husband, right?"

"Yes".

"His name was Harold, remember?"

Then she surprised me by saying, "I miss him a lot".

It's been at least a full year since she's said that. Then she peered at me, and I saw a glimmer of recognition when she told me, "You've been around a long time" and, "Thank you for doing..." She did not know how to finish this sentence, but I took her meaning that she recognized I've been around her for a long time and she appreciates what I do for her. This warmed my heart on such a frigid day. A small window opened up in her brain for a short period of time.

We could not make it to church today due to the snow, and below-zero wind-chill factors, but God came to us with His peace and love, nonetheless.

January 30, 2014

The brutal weather continues, but my heart continues to

warm. I feel a new portion of patience and love. However, Mom's one step forward into a few coherent statements a few days ago has now taken several steps backward, receding into the fog of confusion. She goes into her bedroom in the afternoons, but rather than lying down, she moves items around the room and out of her closet and then comes out to ask me who's been in her room, insistent on the "other" people that are here.

This morning, we were watching a teaching on television about seeking the Holy Spirit and more of His leading, and after the show, Mom made a dismissing gesture with her hands and said "Phooey", like she did not understand a word that was said. I then explained to her what it meant to be born again spiritually and how to receive Jesus's free gift of salvation simply by asking Him to forgive our sins and come into our hearts. We then prayed this prayer together, and when I was done, she said that I "did good". God is very, very good.

11

An excerpt from Mom's memory book:

"My greatest success...I go back to raising my three daughters and being a companion to my husband. We have always tried to be a close family and be together as much as we can. This was my greatest priority in life. This is a success to me."

[Journal entries]

February 8, 2014

It was a busy week, both the days and the nights. Mom's moods and emotions seem to have stabilized since reintroducing her memory medication twice a day. Before Mom moved in with us, Jim and I would eat our meals in the living room in front of the television. Since Mom moved in, we now eat our meals together at the dining room table. How nice it is to share this family time together and have Mom contribute to the conversation, if even in a limited fashion. I see it as a positive way to end a day that may have been rife with mountains of challenges.

I joined a Bible study this week, and it is comforting to draw strength from other women in all walks of life and circumstances. "It is not good for man to be alone". I am learning great teaching. There is peace within.

February 10, 2014

Last night, she was restless, up at midnight, and had quite

a restless day today. Yesterday we went out to breakfast and to church, and even a church function afterwards, but it seems that after a busy day, she expects the next day to be busy as well and keeps asking, "Aren't we going anywhere?" She paced around the house, peering out the windows during each lap around.

Jim has been asked to be the best man at a wedding in Florida in June, so today I had to put my on thinking-cap and develop a plan for Mom's respite care. Both my sisters are not able to help. The first two adult foster care (AFC) homes I called were full and no longer provided temporary respite care. Then I recalled a woman I knew from my years working in the Veterans office who owned several AFC homes nearby. I called her and was blessed to hear her say, "We would be honored to take care of your mom". This is a huge relief.

My plan is to have Mom arrive at the home a week before we actually leave so she can settle in while I am still in town, should any problems arise. Of course, my mind is already spinning with all the instructions to pass along; all the little tweaks we've learned the hard way, such as assistance with toileting, putting lotion on her legs daily to avoid her scratching and causing sores, as well as the assistance I give her at mealtimes. I will spell it all out in writing so no aspect is overlooked. The worry I am experiencing reminds me of the first time I took my toddler son to day care, many years ago. When I left him, he stood at the door and waved at me. I cried all the way to work. Now, Jeff is all grown up with a family of his own. Fortunately, they live nearby and will look in on her at the AFC while I am away. How ironic.

As I look back upon this day, I see that once again, the plans have fallen into place, just when I needed them to.

February 27, 2014

It is just a silly thing really. For as far back as I can remember, Mom has always folded up a tissue with a well-practiced maneuver. She would deftly fold the tissue in halves, into quarters and into eighths, and grabbing it between her thumb and first two fingers, she would tuck it neatly up inside her sleeve near her wrist. There has always been a tissue peeking out of her sleeve, waiting in anticipation of being pulled out and shaken open to its full glory, to dab a drippy nose, or maybe wipe a tear on the faces of her children when they were small. Now, even though so many other memories have been stolen away, that tissue-in-the-sleeve memory holds fast. It is an endearing habit really. They say the earliest memories are the last to leave. I don't know when she began that habit. I could almost picture her own mother tucking a handkerchief up her daughter's sleeve as she sent her off to kindergarten. When I was small, I remember her pulling hankies out of her sleeve. Somewhere through the years, the hankies were exchanged for tissues.

Yesterday, I ran into a little issue with the tissue-in-the-sleeve. I do her laundry, and you may guess where this is going. Sometimes I fail to give her clothes a vigorous shaking out before the load goes into the washer. Oh, I shook the load, and it looked safe, but there must have been a tissue hidden incognito because as the spin cycle ended and I lifted the lid, my worst nightmare was confirmed. The tissue explosion created 3,040,982,698 tiny white bits of wet tissue now sticking like glue to every item of clothing in the washer. This particular load was a cold-water load that had to be line-dried. As I removed the clothes from the washer, some of the tiny bits lost their hold on the clothes and fell on the floor. Those bits will have to be vacuumed up. My plan was to hang the clothes to dry in her bathroom, and then today I took the clothes down and tried to shake the tiny bits off. It looked like snow was falling. More vacuuming. But when I looked at the clothes, there seemed to be just as many tiny bits holding fast.

My new plan (that I thought was a brilliant idea) was to place the clothes in my fancy dryer with the air fluff option, so the tiny bits would drop neatly into the lint tray. As the cycle ended, I grabbed the clothes from the dryer and there were some bits in the lint tray. I then had to wipe down the entire inside of the dryer of errant bits, and some bits fell on the floor (more vacuuming). However, as I carried the clothes into the closet, to my great dismay, I saw the sweaters still carried a slew of tiny bits that were clinging like flies to flypaper. The only recourse was to pick them off one by one and throw them on the floor (which I would vacuum later).

Then the strangest thing happened. As I was picking the bits off the sweaters, it did not seem like I was making any progress because when I turned the sweater around, there were just as many bits on there as before! The explanation was soon apparent. The next tissue piece I picked off and threw to the floor, sailed right back up and landed on the sweater. In fact, I stared in disbelief as the very next tiny bit slipped out of my fingers and appeared to leap right back onto the sweater like it was a magnet. I thought this had to be a joke—some kind of cruel trickery. I sat down and laughed until I cried as I realized that watching that tissue cling to mom's sweaters is just like me clinging to these trivial (but so important to me) lifelong memories that I have of her. Sometimes it seems that is all I have left of her. This was so much more than just a lesson in static electricity. I continued to fight the tiny bits of tissue and finally won. The next time I do the laundry, I will be a little more diligent in shaking and inspecting before turning on the washer, but I will always welcome the fond memories, and a good reason to laugh as well.

12

An excerpt from Mom's memory book:

"My favorite leisure time activity was a lot of things. I have always loved to read, sewing, knitting, crocheting, have always been favorites too. I also do crossword puzzles. In the winter we keep jigsaw puzzles out too. Since Harold retired, my great love is golf. It gets us outside in the fresh air and exercising. It is a great challenge without involving a partner that I might let down, unless we play in a league. My taste in T.V. tends to be mild programs like 'Murder She Wrote', 'Lucy'. The newer ones aren't funny—they are stupid. Don't like all the violence and raw sex or sexist remarks. It is crude. No class. Of course, when I was young there was no T.V. Radio had just gotten its start & was very popular. We had a cottage on Grosse Ile, so the men usually fished & listened to baseball and races on the radio. It didn't seem like the women did much of anything except cook. There are many programs we watch [now], like animal specials, historical, Ancient Bible Times, etc."

[Journal entries]

March 6, 2014

Anxiety levels are rising in the afternoons. The doctor says this is definitely "sundown syndrome", although it is not limited to when the sun actually goes down, because for us, it starts in the early afternoons. Every five minutes, she says "I want to go home", or, "Who are the men that come here?" I'm not sure who the "men" are she is referring to. She mentions her "mother" and her "father" and her "brother", but she no longer knows their names. And, she is still foraging for food. I had to stop her from eating two raw steaks that were sitting on the counter to thaw. She took two bowls out of the cupboard and filled them with water. When I asked what she was going to do with them, she said, "I'm going to take them home". I had to tell her several times that I was her daughter and she lives with me now in our home. She said "Thank you, you are very nice to me". However, she has no concept of what a daughter even is, and of course, there is no recognition today.

Since we have located an AFC home for temporary respite care, Jim and I decided to take a vacation to Myrtle Beach in a couple weeks. She will be housed with other ladies at the AFC home who wander, but are classified as "high-functioning". I think she will enjoy being around the other women.

March 16, 2014

Tomorrow morning, I will be preparing the written instructions for Mom's care during her stay at the AFC home. I must take care not to omit anything important. There is so much care to document, I'm not sure where to begin. I guess I'll start with, "Time to rise and shine", and go from there. On March 20, Wendi will be going with Mom and me for a walk-through visit of the AFC home in the early afternoon, since she and Jeff are the nearest family members while we are gone on vacation. Although it will be interesting to see Mom's reaction to the home, the visit is really more for us than her, because she will not understand why she is there, and she will not remember being there ten seconds after she leaves.

Yesterday, I was upstairs fixing my hair when I heard a loud noise. I looked down to the front hallway and saw that Mom had gone out the front door, down two steps, and was heading down the sidewalk without a coat in twenty- degree weather. I don't even remember running down the stairs; I was moving so fast to intercept her. It is her usual routine to come looking for me if I'm out of her line of vision for two minutes, however; she doesn't usually open the front door and go outside. We have now put a motion-detector alarm on the front porch, to be added to the existing alarms covering her bedroom door, the hallway, and the kitchen. Last night, she came out of her room eight times before 12:30 p.m. She has loads of energy, and mine is zapped.

Tonight, I pulled out her memory book to read because I wanted to see her beautiful handwriting and to swim in the sea of memories she so carefully recorded there. I know it was her wish to have a "quality of life to the end". It was my parents' desire to never become a burden to their children, so my frugal dad saved his pennies and dimes to secure their future. None of us know what our future will look like. Mom would not have chosen the disease that has chosen her. The small blessing is that she is not aware of how much she has lost.

March 20, 2014

It was a whirlwind of a day today following an exhausting week, her fretful behavior accelerating to even new heights. Mealtimes have become a stand-off with her sitting on her hands and refusing to eat. The more I enticed her to eat, the more obstinate she got. She refuses to eat her meals, yet by early afternoon, she anxiously wanders around the kitchen, peering into cupboards and pulling out forks or just whatever she can find. I may have to put gates up to bar her entry into the kitchen (like I saw they had at the AFC home).

She is exercising her vocal cords, with the usual refrains of, "I don't know what I am doing here, I just want to go home," and, "Just give me something to eat so I can go to my room", etc. etc. However, I will take some of the blame because I am the one without the disease, yet my nerves are stretched thin, not leaving much room for self-control. I was running out of tactics in my bag of remedies, and we were at odds. She can no longer read, play games, or walk very far (due to her bad back). Therefore, her main function is sitting and watching television, and I can understand why she would tire of that.

I have been desperately looking for solutions, and today I found one. I visited an adult day care facility in our town, and what a blessing they are. I can drop her off in the morning and pick her up late in the afternoon. She will have company there, and there isn't even a television. She will have interaction among the people and the workers, and even the volunteers, who all seem very kind. I wish I could have found them a long time ago. The plan is to take her there on Tuesdays (so I can get my housework done) and maybe also on Thursday afternoons. This is a god-send.

The second item on my agenda today was our visit to the AFC home with Mom and Wendi. Our vacation is coming up in a couple weeks. It is a lovely ranch home with six other ladies having close to the same level of dementia as Mom. It appeared to be very clean, and the staff was nice. Mom seemed at ease there, she was not paranoid, and she even tried to engage in conversation. My plan was not to tell her today that she was going to stay there in a couple weeks, because that would cause her to be anxious, and she would not remember anyway. The visit just served for her to visit so that when she goes back, she may have some familiarity. The visit went better than I expected.

March 29, 2014

The pacing and agitation have grown epic, with some belligerence thrown in. Mom is no longer satisfied with, as she puts it, "just sitting in that chair". The doctor prescribed a sedative, which I give her after lunch. She has also been rising from bed and going in search of someone several times a night past midnight. She says she wants to go home, and when I ask her where "home" is, she says, "With my mom, and dad, and sisters".

Three more days until she goes to respite care. I think respite will be good for both of us. I am still trying to be wise and kind and redirect whenever possible. It does no good to argue with an AD patient, because no one wins. God's grace allows me to just step back and be amazed, on the one hand, that I even took on this task; on the other hand, the way everything has fallen into place and the help has arrived at just the right time. Even my marriage has grown stronger—His grace cannot be contained. His mercies are new every morning.

13

An excerpt from Mom's memory book:

"I'll never forget the first trip we took to California in 1953. Ronnie was 18 months old, Laurie was 17 months older and Leslie was 5 years. I never enjoyed traveling before, because I hated to sleep in someone else's (motel) bed. But we started out about 4 or 5 o'clock each morning. The girls would sleep for a few hours in the car. Then we stopped about 2:00 in the afternoon so we could swim in the pool & walk & exercise. After that I always loved to travel." [We took one more road trip to California and three road trips to Florida during the 1950's and 60's.] "When the girls were all gone, it was lonesome on the trips. We got more from our trips with the girls, more to see, more to do. We went to Jamaica for our 25th Anniversary. It was nice and beautiful, but that's all. Our first trip to Germany was a very exciting experience. We visited Leslie in Heidelberg & Mannheim. Then we traveled by car to Paris & Luxemburg. Stayed at very quaint hotels because we were traveling by a book, "Traveling Europe on $5.00 a day". Then we had 3 more trips by tours to Europe. They were all very exciting because Harold was born in England. Also, all my grandparents came to America from Germany around 1875."

[Journal entries]

April 1, 2014

The daybreak was cloudy and cool this morning. We began

with our normal routine. I could not bring myself to tell her she would be going to the respite care home today. I felt the right words would come at the right time, but when I found myself driving her there, no words came. I just could not think of what to say. We drove on in silence. I believed that if I told her she was going to stay at respite care for a couple weeks, it is likely she would either: not understand, become anxious, grow agitated, and/or not remember what I told her by the time we arrived anyway. All these excuses were probably true, but that did not make me feel any better. I had a sickening feeling in the pit of my stomach, similar to when you have to take a beloved ailing pet to the veterinary to be euthanized. My nerves were spent by the time we arrived.

Upon entry into the home, I showed her around and got her settled in a chair. I gave the carefully typewritten instructions to the caregiver, gave Mom a hug and a "See you later," and walked out the door. I simply could not come up with a better way to handle the situation without unduly upsetting her, and as it turns out, this was for the best. When I called the home later, she was settling in nicely. I think today was many times more difficult for me that it was for her.

April 10, 2014

A flurry of activity, such as packing, cleaning, and the general whirlwind of preparations take up all of one's mental and physical energy as our vacation draws near. Then, in the blink of an eye, we are driving out our driveway toward our destination. Nine hundred miles later, we arrive safe and sound at Myrtle Beach. Although the weather was somewhat cool, we managed to play golf, eat out (a lot), and take in the sights. Now, six days into our trip, I haven't received any emergency calls, or even any calls with questions, so I have to assume my lengthy written instructions, complete with my "troubleshooting" directions, have served their intended purpose and Mom is being properly cared for.

Wendi was appointed the interim contact person, so I called her today for a status update. She assured me that except for one prescription-ointment question, all was quiet on the home front. Her visits to Mom had gone well, and Mom was eating and sleeping, although there were conflicting caregiver reports about what time she goes to bed. I choose not to worry. God has capable hands.

April 13, 2014

We arrived back home yesterday and I picked up some medications at the pharmacy and took them to the respite home to visit Mom. She looked directly at me and recognized me as the person who was with her every day, but did not remember my name, which is no surprise. She just had a shower before I arrived, so I dried and curled her hair, and she seemed to enjoy this a great deal. As I was preparing to leave, I told her I would see her and take her home in a few days. She then leaned over and whispered, "You can take me with you now". I told her I had some work to take care of first.

I really need to commence my spring cleaning at home since the constant supervision she requires does not lend itself to my being occupied cleaning in another part of the house. Now, as the time draws close for her return, I cannot help but wonder what changes there may be. Will she be glad to come home, or will she need to adjust anew, as she did when she first moved in with us? Will she settle into the routine that became familiar before she left? I'm prepared for whatever comes.

April 18, 2014

Mom came home yesterday. As I arrived at the respite care home, she was anxious to go. Since being home, she seems more content and is not wandering today. What a blessing. I hope it lasts.

April 22, 2014

We are running an endurance race; endurance through a

course of challenges. We must endure this time alone since Julie remains on vacation for yet another week and Jeanne has been in the hospital. Despite my conscious efforts toward a higher level of patience, Mom is resurrecting her vices of wandering and not eating at mealtimes, yet sneaking food the minute I am distracted elsewhere. So today I covered her uneaten breakfast with foil and left it on the counter. True to form, when I was out of the room for a few minutes, I caught her covering the plate back up and chewing voraciously. Aha! Even though it is the same food, I guess she would rather "sneak" it than eat it at mealtime. I don't think I will fret over uneaten meals any longer now that I know what to do with them.

We had a positive experience today during our visit to the adult day care center for her assessment. It is run by a charitable organization. She met the workers, volunteers, and fifteen other dementia sufferers, and she really enjoyed herself. The activities there include seated mild exercise, round-table discussions about the news of the day while they enjoy their coffee, as well as crafting certain art projects and playing games like ring toss, etc. They also eat a good lunch. I believe it is very much like a senior center (only the participants are a little more impaired). Therefore, I'm telling her that she is going to the "senior center," when I drop her off there. She seemed happy on the way home, smiling. I love those smiles. I arranged for her to visit there on Tuesdays. Truly, this is another god-send.

We arrived home at 3:00 p.m. today. She was becoming anxious, so I gave her the prescribed light sedative, and she settled down and ate her entire dinner.

April 23, 2014

Today we went for a walk outside, and she leaned so heavily on her walker that her hands hurt her. Then her anxiety escalated shortly after lunch. Very often throughout the day, she would say, "I want to go home to Detroit". Then she would say, "I need to go to school. I go to Redford High School". On one occasion, I told her that she hasn't been to school for more than seventy years, and she looked at me in total disbelief and bewilderment. It was as if the last seventy years of her life were wiped away; nonexistent.

When I reminded her that she had been married and had three daughters, she said, "Yes, I grew up with them". Again, she has no memory of having three daughters, and no comprehension of what it means to raise three daughters. I have, no doubt, acquiesced to the fact that she hasn't known who I am for quite some time now. Prior to her moving in with us, this occurred so gradually that it would be impossible for me to say when the last day was that she recognized me, and what next day she didn't. Rather, it seemed to occur in fragments. Back when she still lived in her condo, one day she knew me by name and knew I was her daughter. Another day she knew I was her daughter, but could not recall my name. The next day she would call me by name, but could not understand I was her daughter. But now, she only recognizes me as a caregiver that she sees a lot of.

A great deal of time elapsed between each of these milestones; therefore, my heart did not break during such a gradual loss. However, my heart breaks now when I see the confusion in her eyes, the furrowed brow brought on by worry over not being where she thinks she should be, and by the set of her jaw when she becomes angry that I cannot provide the answers to her garbled questions. I can see her trying so very hard to make sense of it all, like trying to identify a person, place, or thing through a dense fog that shifts and lifts for an instant, only to fall back down, covering everything. Her frustration is palpable. She wants so much to hold a normal conversation, she resorts to using her hands to point and gesture what she can't say, like trying to communicate with a person who speaks another language. Most times, I agree, or nod, or just go along with the pantomimes, just so she will believe that I understand what she needs to tell me.

The best part of the day today was when a funny commercial came on the television and she laughed spontaneously, and then I laughed, and we both giggled like schoolgirls. Of course, since she did not remember the commercial even one minute after it ended, the very next time it came on, we laughed all over again. Simple comedies on television are becoming her best friend. I never know what will trigger her to laugh, or how much she understands what she sees, but I'm always ready to laugh along with her.

April 27, 2014

I continue to hone in on the laughter. When she smiles or laughs, even when I am clueless as to why, it doesn't matter; I smile and laugh right along with her. It brightens our moods and lightens our spirits. Yet when the day becomes challenging, I found a scripture verse that reminds me that God will guard me and keep me in perfect and constant peace and I lean on and hope confidently in Him. I never know what tomorrow will bring with my mother. Of this thing, I am sure, she is in His hands and whatever He calls me to do, He will equip me to do, for He will never leave me nor forsake me. It is my hope that if someone else who is despairing of their situation ever reads this, they will find comfort in these words and know they are not alone; otherwise, this would be a very lonely journey, indeed.

April 29, 2014

Today Mom began her regular Tuesday visits at the "senior center" daycare facility from 9:30 a.m. to 3:30 p.m. After the first hour spent signing more paperwork, I went home to commence spring cleaning. The rain was pouring this morning, but by the time I arrived home, it warmed to the seventies and the sun was out, the birds were singing, and all was right with the world (my world, anyway). Ten windows got washed, and there are only twenty-two left to do. There is something therapeutic about cleaning your home. It is good for the soul. When I arrived at the "senior center" to pick up mom, she was smiling and laughing. On the ride home, she said she had a really good time, "But I don't want to go there every day". I said I was very glad she had such a good time and assured her she wouldn't be going there every day.

14

An excerpt from Mom's memory book:

[Regarding her career] "I really had no choice, my father told me I was to do secretarial work and that was that. I had visions of going to college to become a reporter, or to go in the nursing profession. I've always been interested in anything medical. But he wouldn't hear of it. In those days, his word had to be law. I did secretarial work before we were married & for a few years after. My first position was with an advertising agency. I loved it, but the war started and I was able to get a position in a small plant doing defense work. The money was much more. My first job paid $60.00 per month. Of course, that was right after high school. I was also going to business college after work. My positions after that started at $35.00 a week & up. For years, I worked as an election inspector. That got me out of the house once in a while. I also worked as Church Secretary for 5 yrs.

Of course, I think I was and am a very good homemaker and mother, if you can call it a profession. I also sewed all the girls' clothes and my own, the most fun were their wedding dresses. Also, [I] made all the drapes for our homes. Knitting & crocheting was very productive too. When I finish an afghan, sweater, doily, baby things, etc., I feel that I have accomplished something."

[Journal entries]

May 6, 2014

Today Mom had her second visit to the "senior center" daycare facility. The people there seem so nice and told me they played bean bag toss and played UNO and all the while Mom was smiling and laughing. We've come to know, however, that this type of laugh is really just a way to go along with conversation that she doesn't understand and doesn't know how to respond to. As I mentioned, it is rather similar to trying to communicate with someone speaking to you in a foreign language. You respond with smiles and hand gestures while looking for someone who can interpret, or escaping as quickly as possible. Once I got her settled and belted in the car on the ride home, I asked if she had a good time, and she said, "That was awful". Yet, when pressed for details, she could not say what was awful. I will venture a guess that they encouraged her to participate in conversation and activities that were challenging to her and it made her uncomfortable.

Upon arriving home today, she was very restless. After going to bed, she popped back up many times, even getting belligerent with Jim, yet somehow had the insight to come out and apologize minutes later by saying she did not know why, but felt she needed to apologize for some reason. Jim and I agreed we will continue to take her to the center on Tuesdays since it is still better than the boredom and anxiety she experiences while sitting around the house. If they challenge her a little out of her comfort zone, that will be all right. She may come to like it more. Next week could be a whole new experience. Every minute of every day is a study of what works and what doesn't work; like that proverbial "box of chocolates"—you never know what you're going to get.

May 16, 2014

This task could be overwhelming. Although, it is not easy (as most worthwhile ventures in this life tend to be) it is worthwhile to care for my mother in her time of need; after all, if not me, who then? Perfect strangers? I began this journey believing I was doing a noble thing; a sacrifice, if you will. But I no longer view it in that light. With learning so much and gaining so much during this process, how can that be viewed as a sacrifice on my part? In fact, I now believe myself to be rather impertinent to view caring for my mother to be a sacrifice—or even a duty. No, it is a *privilege* I've been blessed with. Not all privileges are easy as we are going through them. It is what we gain in the process and how we come out on the other side that matters. Meanwhile, I stay the course, one day at a time.

Mom's mental condition continues to deteriorate. Afternoons bring with them increased confusion and anxiety. The mild sedative the doctor prescribed seems to only escalate her paranoia. I continue to try taking her for rides in the car. Sometimes, changing her environment helps for a short time, but if she is home, she gets angry because she, "never goes anywhere", and if I take her somewhere, she wants, "to go home". She increasingly says that she wants to go home to her mother. These chants become obsessive as the afternoon wears on. She frets and fusses until she finally says she might as well go to bed. If left to her own devices when I'm busy elsewhere, she goes to her bedroom, pulls clothes out of her closet and towels out of her bathroom, and strews them around her room, sometimes donning clothes, on top of clothes or removing her slacks and putting on two tops, etc.

The best solution I have found is just to help her by removing her shoes and helping her into bed, saying, "Just close your eyes and rest a little while". A gentle word usually works to soothe and calm her.

15

An excerpt from Mom's memory book:

"I'll never forget my wedding day [June 27, 1942]. It was a beautiful day—sunny and 80 degrees. I was frustrated all day just sitting around because they wouldn't let me help with any preparations. My mother, aunts, and sisters were fixing all the food (fried chicken). I wore a chiffon long dress with a finger-tip veil. Harold wore a navy suit. The wedding took place at home and we were officially married at 7:50 o'clock. There were about 100 guests. My father didn't want us to marry then because the war was on. He was afraid Harold would be called up but I insisted because I wasn't afraid. I was very mature for my age "20" and Harold was "21". He worked at [an auto company] on defense work. We were fortunate that he didn't have to go. Of course, he was working long hours—12 hours a day, 7 days a week. I knew after the 2nd date that it would be permanent.

We left the reception at 11:00 p.m. to go to "Johnson's Rustic Tavern" at Higgins Lake [MI]. We had 3 days before going back to work."

[Journal entries]

June 9, 2014

Jim and I just returned from the Florida wedding for the weekend, and today I felt the weariness settle in my bones. The plan was to spend a quiet, restful afternoon with Mom, but apparently, this was not the plan Mom had in mind. It was a beautiful sunny, mild day of about seventy-five degrees, so the doors were open, but the screen doors were locked for safety. Mom tested those doors and grew frustrated when she could not exit. She asked me, "Why do they lock us in here?" She finally managed to unlock the screen door and went out to sit in a chair on the front porch, only to return five minutes later. She then commenced a series of laps around the kitchen, dining room, living room, hallway, and back to the kitchen. Each lap through the kitchen, she would come out with a mouthful of grapes that I had left on the counter for her to find, but when she spied me, her face belied a defiant leer, as if she was just daring me to say she shouldn't eat those grapes.

Due to my weariness, I take some responsibility for the next incident I'm about to tell you. I was denied the nap I so desperately needed, while I was tasked to keep a watchful eye on wandering Matilda, yet trying (but not always succeeding) to be as pleasant as I could be, when I came to realize that she was not coming out of the kitchen. So, once more, I was forced to go and investigate. I discovered her rifling through paperwork and then start to flick through my personal telephone book. Of course, I know she has no comprehension of what she is reading; however, I took the book (maybe a little too abruptly) and simply said, "This is my phone book that belongs in the drawer, so I am going to put it away". She then proceeded to tell me, "You can go to hell". Wow, I'm sure the shock was written all over my face. I tried to convince myself that this was the disease talking, and not my mom talking. I told her she could go to her room because I did not need to be talked to like that. Five minutes later she came out of her room and actually apologized to me. I don't think she remembered the words she was sorry for, but she seemed to sense that she was being nasty and something inside told her this was wrong.

I realize how important it is for me to get my rest, because it takes strength for me to be calm and gentle, and to turn away wrath with a kind word. After all, one bad mood, plus one bad mood, equals one big ugly mess and two very unhappy people.

June 19, 2014

Mom and I both had appointments with our primary doctor yesterday. (We both have the same doctor that we love because she always takes the time to listen and answer all our questions. This is a rare commodity in many of the doctors I have seen.) The appointment was in the afternoon, which is Mom's anxious time, so Mom's agitation began and grew like the dragon emerging from its cave. She was huffing and puffing and speaking inappropriately as the doctor turned to me and said, "I see it must be her bad time of day". This was the first time her doctor has seen this extreme behavior. She prescribed a daily anti-anxiety/depression medication, which should help alleviate these conditions after about three weeks, the time it takes for the medicine to get into her system. The doctor also suggested palliative care (which is hospice care) once again. She said she would sign the order when we decide it is time for this type of help. (Once you sign up for hospice, the hospice doctors take over and Mom would no longer see her primary doctor.) Then we discussed the probability that the hospice doctor will probably discontinue the blood pressure medications, and only continue the medications that make her comfortable.

I felt sick to my stomach during the ride home because I felt that if we took Mom off her blood pressure medicines, this could cause a stroke, or essentially could be a death sentence, and my gut was telling me it wasn't the right thing to do this at this time. Her smiling face stuck in my mind with visions of her laughter and her continued valiant, yet rare efforts to perform normal functions and hold a normal conversation.

When Jim arrived home from work, we discussed this matter, and he put it in the proper perspective for me when he said that she still has good moments, and although she is somewhat picky with her food, she is still eating and definitely enjoying her desserts. Besides that, he said, "I know you; and you would suffer pain and guilt, feeling responsible if she died or suffered from a blood pressure-related malady." This is so true, and I discussed the situation with my sisters as well. They believe I will know when the time is right to call in hospice, and I believe I will know when the time is right. For now, we will continue to give her the best quality of life day by day.

June 28, 2014

Mom has an abscess in her tooth. This will involve several dentist appointments with both the dentist and an oral surgeon. Tomorrow we consult with the oral surgeon, and my huge concern is the anesthetic involved. Mom's devastating loss of memory from the anesthetic administered during her back surgery some five years ago could have a disastrous effect if it happened again. There are certain anesthetics affecting the brain that should not be given to AD or dementia patients, and I learned which ones these are. I printed out the information so I can take it to the oral surgeon in the morning to avoid dire complications.

16

An excerpt from Mom's memory book:

"My spouse [Harold] is tall, 6 ft., had wavy hair when he was young. When he was young, he was quite mild mannered. He thought a lot of his mother. It has been said that the man that has great esteem for his mother will do so for his wife. It seems to be true. He was always a very steady worker on his job, worked much overtime to better our income. Our girls were always a great part of his life. [He] always wants to be on time. Fortunately, he has enjoyed good health. We always have treated one another as a stranger. We've always used "thank you" and "please" to one another. Very dependable. Has always loved to do things with our 3 girls—when they were young, and right through to and in their married lives. The only key to selecting your spouse is that you feel you would not want to live without him. Of course, if he is criminal or abusive, etc., force yourself to live without him. Otherwise, you'll lead a very miserable life. When we were first married, he warned me never to tell him what to do—ask him to do it. It works."

[Journal entries]

July 15, 2014

So much has happened in the last three weeks. I will try to pick up where I left off. I found a good oral surgeon who was familiar with the detrimental effects that certain anesthetics have on AD patients, and he agreed to use a light intravenous sedative. After the surgery, Mom soon woke as her usual self, with no residual problems.

The surgeon and I had a good conversation about AD. He told me that both his parents also had AD, and we talked about the disease having genetic origins. We discussed the new test that has been developed to determine whether someone has the AD "gene" and may be predisposed to acquiring the disease. He said that he would like to take the test so he can take any preventative measures available. It seems to me that those measures would be mainly herbal and lifestyle measures, since there is no medication currently on the market to prevent AD. I told him that I am eating the right foods and taking herbal remedies now, and I will probably not take the test because I would rather not know if that disease is in my future. If I knew I had the gene, every time I misplaced my keys, I would think I was well on my way to AD, and this would cause me to be depressed. I guess it is a matter of choice. If a medicine is developed to prevent or cure AD, the whole situation would change and then I would have to rethink my strategy.

Due to the abscessed-tooth extraction, yesterday I took Mom to her regular dentist for the fitting of her reconstructed lower denture plate. However, the plate did not fit correctly, and another impression had to be made and sent to the lab so they could make a new one. Mom could not follow the dentist's instructions, so I had to "interpret" with visual cues. When he wanted her to open her mouth, I had to open my mouth wide and show her how to do it.

On July 5, my sister-in-law sadly died in Florida, so we made an emergency trip to Orlando. I am thankful for the adult foster care home owner who, once again, agreed to care for Mom on last-minute notice. On the day I returned to pick her up from the home, I was told she was anxious and would not swallow her pills without mixing the pill with some yogurt. The "senior center" also said something about this. Mom's new anti-anxiety/depression medicine seems to be taking some of the edge off her anxiety, but the doctor prescribed another medicine as needed for extreme episodes. I have not administered this one yet, because it tends to make a person somewhat lethargic.

July 19, 2014

For nearly every Sunday since we began caring for Mom thirteen years ago, Jim and I have taken her out for breakfast, as we did this morning. I ordered our usual pancakes, but today we experienced another milestone at the restaurant. She could not eat her pancakes. Not only did I have to cut them up for her, but I had to put each piece on her fork and hand it to her. However, this past week she has not been as anxious. She is not wandering as much, and just appears to be more content. I believe the anti-anxiety/depression medication has taken the "edge" off.

July 27, 2014

It was a long weekend with no caregiver. We took Mom out to dinner on Saturday and out for breakfast on Sunday. Most mealtimes now, she just puts her fork down after a couple bites and stops eating. She doesn't seem to remember how much she ate, and she thinks she's finished. I now have to spear the food with her fork and then hand it to her, and she will eat it if I do this at every meal. She still wandered much of this afternoon and spoke in nonsensical sentences using the wrong words and pointing at objects like tissue boxes, but clearly referring to something else in her mind. Today she had bowel incontinence and did not realize it (another milestone). She is becoming more breathless while walking and has to stop to catch her breath.

Taking her medications is more of a challenge. She keeps them in her mouth and doesn't understand she has to swallow them. I've learned a good trick is to give her yogurt with her pill so she will swallow it. At times she tries to put her pill in her water glass, but I usually catch her. Friday night, I handed her the toothbrush with toothpaste on it and told her to brush her teeth. I turned to put something in the cupboard, and when I turned back, she was brushing her hair with her toothbrush, toothpaste, and all. She has to be watched as closely as a toddler, maybe more so, and sometimes, like today, I get a little worn out. I've aged a bit since the last time I had to care for a toddler every day.

I still treasure the moments we laugh at "The Golden Girls" or some funny commercial on television. When she laughs, it makes me believe that just maybe she isn't suffering too much.

17

An excerpt from Mom's memory book:

"I'll never forget the night when we went dancing at the 'State Fairgrounds' outside under the stars in the moonlight. The music "Flamingo" always reminds me of it. Before we went there, I was introduced to Harold's mother, father, Aunt Alice and Uncle Bob. I remember I wore a dress that had a red print skirt and plain red jacket. I loved it so much [that] I wore that dress when we left our wedding reception. I don't think there is anything as romantic as dancing under the stars on a beautiful warm night."

[Journal entries]

August 10, 2014

It was rather a rough day. Sometimes when Mom and I are watching television, she will say, "I don't know what they're talking about". Today at church, during the message, she said out loud, "I don't know what he is talking about". I had to put my finger over my lips to shush her. This was the first time she ever said something inappropriate at church.

Jim caught her sticking her fingers into the cake this afternoon (because I forgot to hide it as I usually do). Also, this afternoon I had to help Jim to install a light fixture in the upstairs bathroom, yet tried to keep an eye on mom by peering over the railing from the loft since she was in her wandering mode. She just would not stay seated, so every five minutes, I had to go find her. It was exhausting running up and down the stairs.

She requires greater assistance at mealtimes every day now, and tonight she wouldn't swallow her pills without a lot of instruction, which occurs quite often. Whenever I get up to go somewhere, she follows me like she is attached to my hip. I grew so tired today, but I am always reminded that she will not be with me forever, and I appreciate that she is with me now.

August 18, 2014

Three days ago, we had a devastating incident that is going to change everything. It has been a long and eventful last three days. On Friday, Jim and I took Mom to the driving range so we could hit some golf balls and give Mom some fresh air. There is a bench situated behind the tee boxes, so Mom would have a place to sit and watch us. We started to walk across the grass to the bench with me holding her arm, but it seemed as if her legs were getting heavier and heavier, and she began to bend forward more and more until she was nearly doubled over. We stopped a few feet from the bench, and I told her that she needed to stand up straighter. I tried to help pull her up, then before I knew what was happening, she seemed to swing outward away from me and plopped her rear end down on the grass, although I still held her arm and somewhat broke her fall. She did not seem to be in much pain and was soon able to get her feet under her, and we helped her up and over to the bench. She said she was a little sore now, so I was thinking maybe she would have some bruising.

She sat comfortably on the bench, watching us hit the golf balls, even laughing as she said, "That one went far", or "That one wasn't too good", etc. When we ran out of balls a few minutes later, we each got on one side of her and walked her to the car, which she did surprisingly well, despite her being a little achy and her foot being turned out a little. She seemed to have a little more pain as we boosted her up into our SUV, so I began to think that maybe she had a hairline fracture or some such injury, and we should get an X-ray. We drove her directly to the ER, but this time it took a nurse and a wheelchair to get her out of the SUV. Well, who would have thought that the X-ray would reveal a clean break of the top of the femur at the hip which would require surgical repair with a hip replacement. Even the doctor said it was unbelievable how she could walk and not be in more pain with the type of injury she had.

On Saturday, I had discussions with the anesthesiologist regarding the grave consequences of certain anesthetics for AD patients and we settled on a spinal anesthetic. In fact, he told me the anesthetic that detrimentally affects the brains of AD patients is no longer being used. It was taken off the market. That is good to hear.

The surgery was done on Sunday morning. She came through the surgery with flying colors. The orthopedic surgeon advised us that he used a new procedure making the incision in the front of the hip, which did not require cutting any muscle or tendons for installation of the artificial hip, so her recovery should be less complicated. Despite all this good news, little did I know the dark forest we were about to enter was fraught with peril, and we would not find our way to the other side for quite some time.

I spent Friday, Saturday, and Monday nights and days at the hospital. Laurie stayed with Mom during the day on Sunday and through that night. This gave Jim and me an opportunity to go on a shopping spree, but this was not to be a fun shopping spree; this time we had to shop for rehabilitation facilities. The hospital social worker gave me the names of a few local Medicare-acceptable "rehab" facilities. The nicest one was our first visit. It was only a couple years old and filled with windows and light and was very, very clean. We were very optimistic when we walked in the door, but our optimism soon turned to despair when the administrator told us they could not accommodate an Alzheimer's patient if her disease was advanced. Their facility was for more "independent" type of rehabilitation. There would be no one to feed her, and she would have to go to the dining room by herself. As much as I wanted to make it work, it appeared they could not provide the level of care that Mom required, so we sadly left there and traveled to the next one.

This next facility was a nursing home that had been long established, although it had changed names and owners every few years. In stark contrast to the first facility, the minute we walked in the door, our faces were assaulted by the pungent odor of urine. The floors were an asbestos tile commonly used in the 1950's, and I felt the general aura of dirt all around me. There were zoned-out people in wheelchairs strewn here and there, and we could not even locate anyone who worked there. We left rather quickly.

The last facility was also considered a nursing home, and had also been long established. We reservedly walked in the front doors, but this time we were met with plush carpeting in a modern design and a smiling receptionist behind the front desk. (First impressions mean so much.) Off to our left was a small pool with therapy equipment, and best (but not least) is that there was no urine odor. The administrator gave us a tour of the facility, which was very large. This facility provided for all levels of care, and we came to believe it was the best option for Mom.

When I arrived at back at Mom's hospital room on Monday morning, the nurses said they were so glad to see me because Mom had just poured her orange juice all over her breakfast tray, and they brought her a new tray, so could I please help with her meal? There were so many details to oversee, such as paperwork, medications, feeding, fluid intake, etc. She had a fever last night and has been exhibiting angry outbursts. She even hit a nurse in the face today. She could not follow the directions of the physical therapist today, and they had to half-drag her to the chair. Rehabilitation might prove to be a challenge. She simply does not understand or remember what happened to her and why she is in the hospital and why she needs to follow directions.

I had to prepare a list of questions to ask the nursing home/rehab center when we go there tomorrow. The words "nursing home" have an ominous ring to them. It is not where anyone wants to go. It seems to be a black hole for the elderly. I don't think I am alone in thinking that when people go in there, they don't come out alive, or they end up worse off than when they went in. I hope I am wrong. Leslie is coming from out of state tomorrow to help out. Tomorrow will be a busy day and I need to get a good night's sleep tonight.

August 19, 2014

The EMS took Mom by ambulance to the nursing home for her "rehab" today. She could be there for weeks. I arrived before her and helped to settle her in her room. I met the nurse for her hall and explained Mom's AD and how that would complicate her recovery. I further explained that she needed assistance with eating, and our biggest problem is that she will try to get out of bed and fall down when she feels the pain, since she will not remember she had surgery.

As the nurse leered at me, she said, "If she needs assistance with meals, the family will have to do it, because I don't have extra people to help her eat". I was bombarded with further rules and regulations, including the laws that state there cannot be full rails on the beds and they do not allow cameras to watch that she doesn't get out of bed. They simply do not have the staff to watch her all the time. My worst nightmare had come true. I thought she would be well cared for with all the professional help in a nursing home, but this would prove to be no cake-walk for me.

As her advocate, I would have to monitor her medications even closer now since she would be under the care of unfamiliar doctors and nurses. The pain medicine order was written "as needed", and the staff will not give medicine "as needed" unless the patient asks for it, yet Mom does not know how to ask for pain medicine when she needs it, so that is worthless. The pain medicine needs to be prescribed automatically at certain times of the day. By the end of the day, I was overwhelmed, and I cried all the way home. If I thought my job was difficult before, the word has now developed a whole new meaning. Each and every day ahead will find me traveling to the home to be with Mom all her waking hours, twelve hours a day, seven days a week. Fortunately, I will have some relief with our own caregivers.

We have developed a system of keeping detailed notes on our daily visits, which hopefully will result in a seamless transition from caregiver to caregiver so no aspect of her care would be left to chance. Leaving her care to "chance", in actuality, means leaving her care to doctors, nurses and aides who don't know her needs, and who may not have the time to address every aspect of the relationship between her extensive medical conditions and her treatment. We will maintain our vigil at least until we see how well she will be cared for. I feel that this is my duty as her advocate, and is how I would want to be treated if it were me going into a nursing home. The purpose of this nursing home stay is for rehabilitation for her hip replacement, so we have to make sure that she won't end up worse off than when she went in.

August 20, 2014

Thank God for Leslie. She arrived on her white horse with her armor shining and would take the first week's shift at the nursing home, to give me a break. Our caregivers and I will then take over the remaining time of Mom's nursing-home stay. What follows is a summary of our notes taken during her nursing home stay (though I have omitted repetitious notes for purposes of your readability). It should give a pretty clear picture of the day-to-day workings inside a nursing home.

Leslie's Notes:
7:58 a.m. - Mom is awake. She was given her pills in chocolate pudding. Mom holds one in her mouth that is discovered when I go to feed her. The nurse asked if she swallowed them all and mom says "yes", but there is one whole pill in her mouth that I give to male nurse's aide. He says it is a blood pressure time-release, so it can't be crushed. He will find another way to give it. The aide takes her breakfast order and it arrives at 8:50 a.m. The

dietician comes in and gets a few likes & dislikes. Housekeeping comes in. The physical therapist (PT) comes in. The nurse checks Mom's incision and gives mom a foot pillow for her right foot. The shower aides say there will be two showers a week, with a sponge bath daily. The nurse says that the doctor will come by tomorrow to talk to Mom. The PT goes to read mom's chart and has questions regarding weight-bearing and number of assists. The activity director left an August calendar and says he has two weeks to do a "life history" of Mom's interests and hobbies for future activities.

Her blood pressure and temperature is taken and she is found to have a slight temperature so the nurse gives her Tylenol.

Lunch was brought at 1:30 p.m., and I helped her eat. The occupational therapist (OT) brought a picture chart and introduced herself to Mom again. The nurse gave Mom a pain pill. I requested a fall pad to put down by her bed from the nurse's aide, and the aide suggested two foam wedges could also help keep Mom from sliding or getting out of bed after I leave. We put the wedges in, and they help! I leave when Mom falls asleep after nighttime pills.

August 21, 2014

Leslie's Notes:

8:00 a.m. - Mom is dressed and in a wheelchair. Her pills come crushed in the pudding. I feed Mom her breakfast, cutting up the pancakes. The aide combs Mom's hair and puts her dentures in. I ask the aide to cut up her breakfast food from now on so she can feed herself if we aren't here.

Mom's niece and her husband come to visit just after Mom returns from physical therapy. She was able to stand a little with assistance (in PT). Mom had been taking pain pills regularly for her back pain, and now with the pain from recent surgery, I requested a pain pill for Mom, but the nurse checks the chart and it says "Only as needed" (still), so we need to ask the doctor about ordering a pain pill for the three times a day, as she was getting before the hip break for her back pain. We order lunch.

1:30 p.m. - The dietician says we can plan ahead Mom's lunches on Sunday. I'm waiting for the doctor, so I ask the receptionist if she knows if the doctor is around. She states he left the building at 3:00 p.m. I am puzzled because I was waiting to talk to him to ask him three questions:

1) Do we need a written prescription to add a stool softener daily?

2) Can he prescribe the pain medicine a set three times a day for her back pain (rather than "as needed"), which will also help with her surgical hip pain?

3) How often does he (the doctor) come to see Mom?

I asked the nurse question #3, and she said he comes on Mondays and Thursdays. If needed, the receptionist says we can speak to the head nurse who is here daily. The foot pillow is gone, so a male aide gets another. The dietician will consult with us this weekend for Mom's food order (standing), so be thinking about a standing order as preplanned menu. I brought in hangers and three pairs of Mom's pants. I ordered dinner, and Mom is getting anxious around 4:30 p.m. to "go home". She tries to get out of bed. I pressed the call button, and the nurse came and talked to her, offering hot chocolate, and she says yes, but she only takes a couple sips.

They also did a bladder-retention test on Mom today to make sure she is emptying her bladder (like an ultrasound; it is painless). Dinner comes at 5:30 p.m.

*Note: bring cushion for wheelchair tomorrow. Mom is anxious; she is trying to get out of bed. The nurse gets her up in the wheelchair and gives her the nighttime pills a little early to calm her down and this helps. The fall pad is down (next to bed) and wedges are installed to help prevent her from trying to get out of bed. I leave 7:30 p.m.

August 22, 2014

Leslie's Notes:

8:30 a.m. - I brought in the cushion for the wheelchair, and it fits well. The nurse says Mom will get pain pills three times a day, at 8:00 a.m., 2:00 p.m. and 8:00 p.m., and the stool softener once a day. This morning I had to press the call button because Mom is trying to get up by herself. Mom would not know when to push the call button, or for that matter, what it even is. It would benefit all concerned if they had another system for Alzheimer's patients, such as a regular toileting schedule, rather than relying on call buttons that don't work for patients who don't know how to use them. If we were not here to monitor her bathroom breaks, it appears she may be left to sit in her own waste because there is no follow-up system.

We go to dining room for lunch. Her temperature is taken, and it is slightly elevated. PT is scheduled for 4:00 p.m.

About 1:30 p.m., we go to the hair salon for a shampoo and set. We cruise around, pushing her wheelchair to the library to look at the birds and the fish, and then we go back to her room for rest before PT. Her crushed pain pills and other meds were given at 2:00 p.m. in a pudding. I gave her dirty clothes to the aide to drop off in the laundry. The aide says they'll be delivered back tomorrow.

Mom is taken to PT by me at 4:00 p.m., and she comes back a little tired. We sit in the main hallway at a table. She has on the blue non-skid slippers they gave her. She has dinner in the dining room at 5:30 p.m. and eats about half, but back in her room Mom starts saying she wants to go home. I push the call button, and the nurse's aide transferred her from the wheelchair to the bed. We put the fall pad and wedges in place for nighttime. The aide says he will bring long rectangle pillows to place on both sides of Mom. These will help her to "remember" to stay in bed, along with the wedges. I tuck the sheets around them and under the mattress to help also. Mom gets her pills from the nurse at 7:30 p.m., and I ask the nurse if she can have them at 7:00 p.m. from now on to help her calm down from the anxiousness. The aide brought ice cream. Her blood pressure is very good today (127/62). I leave at 7:35 p.m.

August 23, 2014

Leslie's Notes:

8:30 a.m. - Mom is up, dressed and done with breakfast when I arrive. She has coffee in front of her, but seems to have lost the taste for it. She doesn't have her glasses on, so I found they had fallen off the back of her nightstand. The nurse's aide tells me Mom had a shower this morning. Good.

The head nurse tells me Mom got out of bed unaided at 6:30 a.m. this morning. She says the only solution may be to have someone (family member?) "camp out" with Mom to make sure that doesn't happen again, until she is able to walk and go home. Isn't this their job? Now we're supposed to spend the night here, as well as all day?

We read magazines in the hall. The nurse says that a patient must sit in a wheelchair at the hall intersection table if they try to get up unassisted. (I guess this is their way of keeping a closer eye on them, but it seems like a punishment to me.) Mom is getting anxious starting at 10:00 a.m., she wants to keep asking the time. I push her around the building to relax her, and we go by the therapy room to see what time her PT is today. The physical therapist says Ruth is not scheduled for today (Saturday), that patients go six times a week. This must be Mom's day off. I try to distract Mom with going to lunch, and she eats about half her meal. I brought my own. There is a written standing meal order to cut her meat in small pieces (good).

Despite me pushing Mom in her wheelchair up and down the hall and back to library, she is increasingly agitated, saying she, "wants to go home". She is now stopping people in the hall, asking them to help her get to Detroit, by bus or car, it doesn't matter. She asks over and over, "Why can't I go home?" She says she will walk home and she means it. She is also saying that she, "wants to die". I roll by the nurses' station to see if she can calm her down some. She talks to her. I ask for a sedative of some kind. I have never seen her so anxious—she is kind of trembling. Then she says her back hurts and she would like to lie down. Her pain is increasing, so I ask the nurse for a pain pill. It's only 1:30 p.m., but the nurse agrees, and Mom gets the pill. I ask how long the pill takes to work and the nurse says thirty minutes. Mom settles down and calms a lot, lying in bed with two pillows under her head. The nurse asks me how long does Mom wear her nitroglycerin patch at home, and I tell her overnight. She tells me they take it off at night, but she doesn't know why the change in hours.

The aide changes Mom's brief. The nurse tells me Mom's incision looked good and is healing well (she saw this at the morning shower). The head nurse tells me and Mom that she is going to walk soon. By 3:15 p.m., Mom is quiet and is watching television. Her right ankle looks a little swollen today.

We go to dining room for supper, and she eats less than at lunch. She requires reassurance constantly today that she can go home soon, but not today. She is very anxious. We watch television. I have to press call button four times in a row for toileting, and then she finally lies down. Pills finally come at 7:20 p.m., and she goes to sleep at 7:45 p.m., so I leave at 8:00 p.m.

August 24, 2014

Leslie's Notes:

I call the main phone number on my cell phone to unlock the front door for Ronnie and me at 6:30 a.m., and we get let in. Mom is still asleep. Someone has to be with her all day so she doesn't get out of bed without assistance. There are not enough nurses and aides to watch her all the time, and she always wants to get up and walk to use the bathroom, or to go home, forgetting she had surgery. When we push the call button (because she would not know how to do that), it takes thirty minutes for the aides to respond. It is a dangerous situation.

She wakes at 8:00 a.m. today. She eats a good breakfast in the room. The nurse checks her incision and says it looks good. Her temperature is normal, good! We found out there is no PT today. The area is closed (Sunday). We met up with the physical therapist, who said we would receive a visual chart with exercises on it for the days she is off PT. Mom is dressed by the aide, and we head to library to watch birds. Ronnie leaves.

Mom eats a good lunch at the table in hall. Julie arrives to visit, and I give her a tour. She will arrive at 9:00 a.m. on Monday for caregiving.

At 3:30 p.m. after a snack, Mom is sore and wants to lie down. I press call button, and the aide gets her into bed. Her dinner is brought to her room today about 5:15 p.m., and she has a good appetite. Her granddaughter Nola called and was able to do Facetime with Mom and Nola's son, Asher (age two and a half) who was dancing for me and Mom—so cute.

At 7:00 p.m. I request a small cup of ice cream for mom from the aide because she is getting anxious about "going to her bedroom". We are waiting for the aide to change her into her P.J.'s and also waiting for night pills. Nurse came at 7:20 p.m. after I asked for night pills. Her temp is slightly elevated. The lights are off and she is talking @ 8:05 p.m., but asleep at 8:15 p.m.

August 25, 2014

Ronnie's Notes:

Nellie (my dog) and I arrived at 6:30 a.m. Mom is awake and the aides are working on the lady in the next bed over. At 7:05 a.m., the aides got mom toileted and dressed. They weighed her—181 (minus the wheelchair weight of 35.08) = 146??? This doesn't seem right, it is too high. I will check her previous weights with the nurse. The aide will tell the kitchen to bring her breakfast.

At 7:50 a.m., I asked the nurse when the doctor would be here, and she said he probably wouldn't see Mom today. I could feel my blood begin to boil, so straining to keep my words even, I said he didn't see her last Thursday, either, and we must talk to him today because we have lots of questions. She said what are the questions—she can ask him. I said, "I'm concerned about her slight fever that could be even higher but for the Tylenol bringing it down. Is this a sign of a serious problem?" She said it might be dehydration. I said I was concerned about post-surgery infection, but she said the urine looks good, so there is probably no UTI. If there is no indication of infection, the doctor will not give antibiotics unless he knows what he's treating (maybe if he actually came to see her, he could figure that out). She also will ask the doctor (at my request) for a sedative for Mom and also whether it's okay to move nighttime meds up to 6:30 p.m. due to sundowner's and her usual schedule of early bedtime. She said the doctor will be here between 1:00 and 2:00 p.m. She said Mom's weight yesterday was 126, so she agreed with me that today's weight is not correct, and she will re-weigh her. They finally brought breakfast at 8:30 a.m., and the nurse gave her the morning meds at 8:40 a.m.

Julie's Notes:

Ruth had PT at 9:20 a.m. and OT at 10:15 a.m. She came back to her room at 10:40 a.m. The aide got Ruth in bed, and she went right to sleep, taking a couple catnaps before noon—short but sleeping sound. The nurse came in to meet with Ronnie, and I told her I am the caregiver. She says not to worry on the slight fever, it is normal post-surgery and her white blood count is trending down which is also a good sign. She will talk to the doctor about the night meds being given at 6:30 p.m., but she does not see a problem with that. She will also check with the doctor regarding an anxiety medicine for past noon to ensure Ruth's safety about getting out of bed or chair and anxiously "wanting to go home". Lunch was ordered for Ruth at 12:10 p.m.

Ronnie's Notes:

The doctor was just here. He confirmed what the nurse told Julie—a sedative was not on the list sent over from hospital, but I told him it is on the list her doctor faxed over prior to surgery. The nurse practitioner put it on her list daily for 3:00 p.m. after it is delivered tomorrow. Lunch came at 1:05 p.m.

The nurse transferred Mom from the bed to the wheelchair, and mom did very well. At 2:00 p.m., the activities director came in and asked us scads of questions about likes/dislikes, sports, and interests, etc. He gave me the activity schedule for August.

At 3:00 p.m., Mom is VERY anxious this afternoon. She keeps repeating, "I want to go home" (over and over, etc.), "I need to see my mother", "Does my mother know where I am?," "Is my mother okay?." Dinner came at 5:15 p.m. The aides took her to the bathroom and put her in bed at 5:40 p.m. I rang the call button at 6:20 p.m. because Mom wanted to sleep. Nighttime pills came at 6:40 p.m. Mom seems comfortable.

August 26, 2014

Ronnie's Notes:

I arrived at 6:40 a.m. The aides got Mom up and dressed and in a wheelchair. I combed her hair and took her to breakfast in the dining room at 8:30 p.m. The OT came and took her down to therapy. She also had PT. For a pre-scheduled meeting, Jim and I met with the care management nurse and two OT's. No PT was there. (I was looking forward to meeting with the PT so we could know a timeline for treatment.) The OT went and asked the PT, and she related it would be about two weeks, or maybe a little longer. I took her to the dining room for lunch at 12:15 p.m. She did not eat much. Jeanne is here at 1:00 p.m.

Jeanne's Notes:

Ruth laid down at about 2:30 p.m. She wanted to get up at 3:00 p.m., so I called the nurse to help her. I took her to play Bridge-O and she understood it somewhat, but not completely. The nurse delivered a pill at about 3:15 p.m. while she was playing the game. The aide came and told us they may not let anyone eat in the dining rooms tonight because there's a bad storm outside with high winds and they didn't want any residents by the windows. After a while, they came back and said the storm had blown over so we could go to the dining room. Ruth had been really agitated and wanting to eat, so we finally made it to the dining room.

She then wanted to go to bed so I pushed the call button and the aide got her into bed at 6:00 p.m. She put the wedges, pillows, and the fall pad in place and lowered the bed. I sat with her until she fell asleep, turned the lights out, and shut the door. The aide came in at 7:00 p.m. to get the roommate ready for bed and Ruth woke up then for a few minutes. A few minutes later, the nurse came in and gave Ruth her night meds, and then she went back to sleep again. She woke up again at 7:30 p.m. when the nurse came to give the roommate her meds, so I stayed to make sure she was asleep. She woke again at 7:45 p.m. just when I was about to leave. So, I stayed till 8:00 p.m.

August 27, 2014

Ronnie's Notes:

I arrived at 6:30 a.m. The aides were working on Mom's roommate, and when they finished with her, they took Mom to the shower, got her dressed, and ready for the day. I wheeled her to breakfast. She didn't eat much before she said she was full. We came back to her room at 8:00 a.m. to watch "The Golden Girls" and to wait for her meds and Julie. The housekeeping staff is very efficient. Mom's bed is always changed by the time she returns from breakfast. This nursing home is very clean. That is one big plus, although by now I've come to realize that nursing homes seem so impersonal and inconsistent and they do not seem to know of the special needs of Alzheimer's patients. The staff is rotated from ward to ward. In my opinion, it would be far better if she could maintain the same staff that know her and are aware of her needs and limitations.

The nurse brought her pills at 8:20 a.m. She would not swallow the blood pressure pill, which is a capsule and cannot be crushed. We had to give a lot of water and two cups of applesauce before she finally swallowed it.

Julie's Notes:

At 8:30 a.m., the dietician came in to review food likes and to see how things are going. I got updates from Ronnie, and then she left at 8:45 a.m. Ruth is watching television as I review this notebook, and then I took Ruth for a long walk. The OT was here, and she tried a couple of devices for Ruth to use to take off socks and shoes, but I had to tell her that Ruth would not remember. The OT gave the following instructions on things NOT to do:

No crossing legs

No bending over (i.e. to take off shoes/socks)

No twisting legs/hips

They will also assess how she is lying in bed and make therapeutic/equipment adjustments to ensure she is resting in bed straight. The OT took her down for therapy for arm-strengthening exercises. The PT advised she will be back for more work in the p.m. We went for another trip all around facility. Ruth keeps saying she wants to go home. We came back to her room at 11:15 p.m. and did a few exercises and flash cards on return to her room. We ran into the PT on our walk, and they said they will come to get her after lunch.

I took Ruth to the small dining room at 11:45 a.m. and I brought ice water back to refill her bedside Styrofoam cup. Her pain pill was given right after lunch. At 12:15 p.m., we came back to her room, and I brought back fresh and dry bib as the one in her bedside drawer was kind of wet.

Ronnie's Notes:

I returned at 12:30 p.m. and I pushed call button at 12:40 p.m. for toileting, and they finally came thirty minutes later! Too late! Mom was getting restless, so I took her down to PT at 2:00 p.m. She walked with a walker—one hundred steps! Also, she did very well with OT. At 3:00 p.m., I took her to bingo, and she required much assistance with that. We returned to her room at 4:00 p.m. I told the nurse she needed the 3:30 p.m. sedative, and she thought "she already gave it to her", but five minutes later, she came back and gave her the pill (guess not).

Wendi's Notes:

I took Grandma outside to the courtyard. She said she was <u>so glad to be outside.</u> We enjoyed the outdoors until 5:30 p.m., and then she wanted to go inside. She said she needed to go to bathroom, so I called the aide. It took about fifteen minutes for her to arrive, and she got her ready for bed by 6:00 p.m. At 6:30 p.m., the meds were given. The lady next to her had to be put into her bed with a lift, and Grandma got real nervous when the machine was wheeled in front of her. I told her it was okay and it wasn't for her but for the other lady.

With both televisions going, I don't know how she can relax to sleep. It seems too loud. It is 7:00 p.m., and she's wide awake. I think she is nervous about them tending to the other lady. I pray God will heal Grandma and get her out of here. At 7:10 p.m., she needs toileting, and the aide arrives at 7:25 p.m. By now, Grandma is very agitated. She wants to go to her bed to sleep. I keep telling her this is her bed and it's okay. I called the nurse, and she brought some warm blankets to put on her. At 8:00 p.m., it finally looks like she is asleep, but I will wait a bit to make sure.

August 28, 2014

Ronnie's Notes:

I arrived at 6:35 a.m., and Mom is still in bed. I asked if she wanted to get up and she said, "No". She closed her eyes and went back to sleep, so I let her sleep until 8:00 a.m. and then woke her up. I called the aide to get her up and dressed. Mom seems more confused this morning. I let the aide take her to the dining room for breakfast to see how she does without me. When I looked in on her fifteen minutes later, she was just sitting there, not eating. I told the nurse that Mom was not eating, and she sent an aide to help her—to assist and to give her "cues".

After breakfast, we sat outside in the courtyard for thirty minutes. It was a sunny, brisk, and beautiful morning. She loved it. I spoke to the unit manager and explained how agitated Mom was getting in the evenings with all the commotion surrounding her roommate and that she becomes very alarmed and fearful when they bring in the lift, etc., so I asked if she could be moved to a quieter room with a window bed, so there will not be a continual army of aides walking back and forth in front of her bed. This was arranged, and by lunchtime, she was moved to another room.

The OT came in just before lunch for some therapy, and she then took her to lunch. I spoke to the aide who assisted with breakfast, and it appears she ate a healthy breakfast once she got assistance. The aide suggested "restorative therapy" (or RT), which is a group of therapists whose job is to re-teach her how to eat—and the OT said she will put the request in for that. They will help her with breakfast and lunches only during weekdays. (Now I am really confused as to why the nurse told me on my first day here that the family would have to help with meals because she did not have the staff for this. She had to know about restorative therapy.) I believe it was good that I had my dog, Nellie, with me today, and I could not go in the dining room, because it gave the staff the opportunity to see that she needed eating assistance (this was my secret plan all along).

After lunch, she went to speech therapy and PT. While Mom was in therapy, I was walking Nellie in the hall and was stopped by a delightful couple who said they used to have a Maltese. During our conversation, they told me their ninety-year-old mother resided there in the nursing home and while she has been there, she had fallen twelve times! How is that possible? I would think that after someone fell once or twice in a nursing home, the cause would be determined, and measures would be put in place to assure it would not occur again. This only serves to confirm that our extended presence is needed to protect Mom. I cannot trust her solely to their care if I want her to walk out of here someday soon.

I returned to Mom's PT session and learned that she stood for about five minutes and then had two walking sessions with a walker before growing tired. We went to bingo, but she said she couldn't hear the numbers and got frustrated, so we left.

A woman doctor who seemed nice and very helpful, came in to talk to me. We discussed Mom's history, and she questioned why her primary doctor prescribed both an anti-anxiety/depression med, as well as a similar type of med for sleeping. I explained that the similar med was just for sleeping and the anti-anxiety/depression med really helped her in the afternoons with sundowner's to calm her a bit, and they are both important. I told her I really didn't think the additional sedative that was prescribed here was doing much for her agitation. She asked if we ever tried another sedative, and I said "no, we hadn't". She suggested we give half of the sleeping med dose in mid-afternoon, and then give her usual dose for sleeping with the nighttime pills. She will also prescribe a sedative as needed for agitation (she will word the order so there is no problem to ask for it if she needs it).

At 2:30 p.m., Mom is getting a little antsy, so we went out to the courtyard. After twenty-five minutes, Mom began asking, "When are we going?," so we went back in. As we were passing the nurse, she asked how she was doing, and I told her, "Starting to get antsy". She said the doctor ordered the change in medications, but they didn't have the pills yet, so she gave her the sedative that didn't work so well. Mom laid down for an hour and seem to feel better, but started wondering when we "would go". I took her to dinner and ate with her in the dining room about 5:00 p.m. She needed prompting. After dinner, she wasn't ready for bed, so we sat outside in the courtyard for thirty minutes, then she got her pills and went to bed. She fell asleep, and I left at 7:25 p.m.

August 29, 2014

Ronnie's Notes:

Unfortunately, this place has now become my "home away from home". I arrived a little later today at 7:00 a.m. since mom was still sleeping at 6:30 a.m. the last two days, but who knew, she was up, dressed, and sitting by the nurse's station with the nurse. I left Nellie in Mom's room and took Mom to the dining room for breakfast. At 8:30 a.m. we went outside for fifteen minutes, but it was still a little chilly, so we came back in.

The laundress brought back two shirts, but there are still items of clothing missing. I was sent down to Lost & Found in the therapy room and found one missing shirt and one pajama bottom. I described the still missing articles of clothing to the laundress, but I think I'll take her laundry home and do it myself from this point on—it will actually be less work for me.

It is 9:45 a.m., and no OT or PT yet—so I did the following exercises with mom: toes up (20x) heels up (20x), knee squeezes (20x), left knee lift and kicks (20x each). I had her stand up for three minutes. I had her sit/walk (in her wheelchair) forward out of her room and backward into her room. I walked down to check on her hair appointment and learned it is at 2:00 p.m. We watched game shows until noon when Jim came and picked up Nellie.

I took Mom to lunch, and we ate in the sitting room. The OT was ready for her at 1:00 p.m. after lunch, and then the speech therapist began working with her. Mom was complaining of having pain, so I went to check with the nurse to see if she had her noon pain pill, and she hadn't. The nurse was not aware the doctor changed it to noon, but the unit manager was there and confirmed meds should be given at 8:00 a.m., noon, and 6:00 p.m. I told the nurse, also, a half-dose of the sleeping med was added for late afternoon and she confirmed on the computer it was to be given at 4:00 p.m. but said the usual dose for bedtime was not on there. I said that was incorrect, the half dose, was IN ADDITION to the usual dose at bedtime. She called the doctor and the doctor confirmed this. (An advocate is so important to prevent miscommunications which could lead to disaster.) We also discussed the new sedative that was prescribed which is an antipsychotic, but also acts as a mood stabilizer. At 3:45 p.m., the nurse was very apologetic about not seeing the med change and gave Mom her half-dose of the sleeping med. At 4:00 p.m., mom is on the move in her wheelchair and doesn't seem interested in television. She is getting agitated. She is putting her head in her hands, sighing, etc. Says she wants to go to bed. The aide got her in bed and will ask the nurse for the sedative.

I just noticed that Mom's brown afghan from home is missing off her bed. The aide thinks it may have been bundled up with all the bedding from her old bed and taken to laundry. I told her it was priceless to us because Mom crocheted it with her own hands. She will check with laundry and let me know. I may need to follow up.

Jeff's Notes:

Grandma ate half of her dinner, and on the way back to the room, the nurse gave her the medication. At 6:05 p.m. I rang the aide button to get her ready for bed time. The aide came at 6:35 p.m. (it took thirty minutes for her to arrive). Grandma asked many times, "When can I go home?" The aide got Grandma ready for bed. She was real friendly and took great care of Grandma. Grandma and I watched television for a few minutes, and she fell asleep at 7:05 p.m. I will be leaving at 7:20 p.m.

August 30, 2014

Ronnie's Notes:

I arrived at 6:55 a.m. No one is at the front desk to open the door. I called several times and let the phone ring 100 times (no voice mail?). I knocked and knocked until my knuckles hurt —no one came. I left to go to a fast-food restaurant around the corner and I was finally let in when I returned at 7:30 a.m. I told them the doorbell was broken and the phone rings & rings with no option to dial an extension. They made no comment.

Mom is still in bed—she is VERY depressed—she doesn't want to get out of bed. I have never seen her so depressed before. I can usually talk her into getting up—could it be the new sedative she got yesterday? I pushed the call button with no response, but 10 minutes later, two aides arrived. They didn't seem to be aware that she gets a shower today, so I had to tell them she gets a shower on Wednesdays and Saturdays and they took her to the shower. I completed the menu sheet for the next week. Mom returned dressed at 8:40 a.m. I had previously told the staff that Mom was uncomfortable with a male aide dressing her, so we requested female aides only. The aide told me today they only have a male nurse and a male aide, so when Mom needs toileting or dressing, they will have to call female aides from another wing so it might take a little longer. I can understand that.

After watching television for a little while, we went for a hallway stroll looking for the lost afghan down in the therapy room, but it was not there. We went outside to the courtyard, and she got the biggest kick out of watching the ants scurrying across the cement. It was so cute, she calls them "those little ones". It was good to see her smile again. Returning to her room, housekeeping came to tell us they found the afghan, put her name on it, and brought it back. (Bless them.)

I helped Mom with some PT exercises: toe lifts, heel lifts, knee squeezes, and knee pushes. Then I stood her up, and she walked with her walker around her room one-and-a-half times, with me pulling the wheelchair behind her. She did very well. Since it usually takes a half hour for an aide to arrive after pushing the call button, I decided to take her to the bathroom myself. The transfer went relatively well, since I've watched the aides do it. Mom had lunch at 11:45 a.m., a pain pill at noon, and by 12:15 p.m., she is back in the room and already starting her usual mantra, "I want to go home".

Jeanne's Notes:

We watched a Bob Hope movie. She kept asking what was happening so I would explain it to her. Then she started saying that she wanted to go to bed, so I figured her back was probably hurting. I called for a nurse to come and make her bed. She laid down for a nap at 2:30 p.m.

She started getting belligerent at 3:30 p.m. She said she's not hungry so she's not getting up for supper. She just wants to go to bed now. She said she wants to do what she wants to do. Luckily, the nurse came in at 3:45 p.m. and gave her the half pill! The pill seems to be helping her mood some.

At 4:10 p.m., I buzzed for the aides because she had to go to the bathroom. Twenty minutes later, no one came because they were busy helping people get ready for supper, so I took her and helped her through the process. After eating supper, the aide came in and readied her for bed, but we couldn't find any pajamas, so they put her to bed in her clothes.

The nurse came in and gave her the night meds at about quarter to six. She said it seemed like Ruth was agitated, so she brought her another pill to calm her down. I'm not sure what it was because the nurse had an accent and I couldn't understand her. At 7:30 p.m., she tried to get up herself and wasn't going to wait for anyone to help her. I helped her dress in her pajamas so she'd be more comfortable for sleeping. Since she came back from supper, she hasn't been tired. It's 7:55 p.m. now, so I'm hoping she'll be comfortable enough to go to sleep. I put the fall pad down by her bed and put the pillows on each side of her. It looks like she's going to sleep now. I'll wait till 8:15 p.m. to be sure she's sound asleep before I go.

August 31, 2014

Ronnie's Notes:

I arrived at 7:30 a.m. Mom is very ready to get out of bed, so I rang for the aide. A male aide came in and said he would go to get a gal, who then responded very quickly to prepare her for the day. I took her to breakfast. She seems in good spirits today, although eating her breakfast took much prompting. When the nurse gave her the medications after breakfast, she had trouble, but finally got it down.

At 9:20 a.m., a man came in who identified himself as the physical-therapy doctor. He had her stand so he could look at her incision and pronounced that it looks good. He asked about her memory (none) and her eating (poor). He said the brain tells her she's full, so she doesn't want to eat. He said it would be helpful to put her on a mainly liquid diet at this time, protein shakes, etc. I think this is a great idea—less stressful for her and for us. He will talk to the nurse practitioner about a nutritionist.

9:40 a.m. - I helped Mom do her PT exercises and then had her walk forward and backward (in her wheelchair) and then she walked around her room with the walker twice before tiring. At 10:30 a.m., I took her outside to sit in the courtyard for a while. It is a nice, peaceful and windless day. We watched the ants and their antics again. God is good.

Julie's Notes:

11:50 a.m. - Ronnie gave me updates before she left. I assisted with Ruth's hygiene regime, and the nurse gave her a pain pill. She ate a healthy lunch. We went out to the courtyard for a while after lunch, and then to the library. Ruth does not want to play bingo. She seems to be enjoying "quieter" spaces today. At 2:30 p.m., after the library, she says she is tired. We got back to the room after a short ride around. She walked some with her walker. She wants to lean over too much; otherwise, she did well.

At 2:45 p.m., she took a short nap. A female aide is in at 4:25 p.m. after a young man came in and asked if it was okay for him to toilet Mom and I told him it has to be a female (don't they have our directions written down somewhere?) I averted a major problem when the female aide left Ruth on the toilet, and I overheard her tell Mom to pull the chain that would let them know when she was done. If I was not here to help Ruth finish up in the bathroom, she would not know to pull the chain, she would try to get up by herself, and most likely would panic and fall.

After her nap, all exercises were done, including some arm exercises to strengthen, as well as walking with the walker, and then she ate all of her dinner.

The nighttime meds were done at 6:00 p.m., and the nurse asked if the agitation pill was needed. I told her that yes, since dinnertime, Ruth has been very frustrated and wanting to go home, despite multiple walks and more exercise, no diversion seems to work. She is just despondent with me on this rare occasion. The nurse will have the aides get her ready for bed. The male came in again—automatically asked if I want a female—I smiled and said yes. At 6:30 p.m., a female aide got Ruth's teeth brushed, dentures soaking, pj's on, bed wedges in place and fall pad down. Ruth must be very tired, as just minutes later, her eyes are closed and she is very calm. I will stay awhile to be sure she's still sleeping. She is still asleep at 7:00 p.m. – has not awakened – so I am heading out.

18

An excerpt from Mom's memory book:

"I'll never forget meeting Harold for the first time. I was on a Detroit News Hike. He came to visit with a friend of his. After we hiked, we always stopped at a tavern to eat and dance. I fell over Harold's feet as he had them stuck out while sitting. At that time, all the cars the kids owned were pretty old. After we ate, my girlfriend Marge and I went to the car to put on some lipstick. After we put on our lipstick, we couldn't get out of the car. It was parked next to a hedge. The other door on the other side had its handle broken inside, so it would only open from the outside. Harold was leaving & passed so we asked them to open the car door for us. We started to talk & they said they would come out to visit next Sunday. That Sunday we made a date to go dancing on the following Saturday, then another the week after. Then we went steady for 1 ½ years."

And so the long days continued at the nursing home throughout the whole month of September. Each day brought new challenges, and changing staff. We continued to maintain notes to coordinate her care. Although this coordination and trading of information was vital to prevent tumbles, mishaps, medication misunderstandings, and generally keeping her safe at the nursing home, it could be tedious for readability. Therefore, what follows are relevant notes from only a few more days in the nursing home:

September 4, 2014

Ronnie's Notes:

When I arrived at 7:15 a.m., I had to ring the doorbell because no one was at the front desk. Mom was up, dressed and sitting at the hallway table (where the nurse could keep an eye on her), so we went to the small dining room, and waited for the RT to bring her breakfast, which she ate with much prompting. While she was eating with the therpist, I asked the nurse for a "scoop" or "concave" mattress that I learned about to help Mom to stay in bed. It is curious why I had to suggest this to the nurse, rather than the nurse suggesting this to me, since the nurses are well aware of Mom's propensity to get out of bed without assistance. The new mattress was brought by maintenance about thirty minutes later. This should work well, but I will continue to put wedges in the openings on the side.

September 9, 2014

Ronnie's Notes:

I arrived at 7:25 a.m. Mom is up, dressed and sitting at the table in the hall, looking at a magazine and drinking coffee out of a cup with a sippy top. The problem is, no one gave her a clothing protector, so she has five coffee stains all down the front of her white shirt. Breakfast was ordered, and the RT helped her eat (about 75%); then I took her right down to do OT and speech therapy. They also worked with side-stepping, and did the arm bike. She seems a little tired today and is struggling a little more finding her words. I brought her back to her room to wait for the therapist to come get her for PT and "gait training" for me. This training will show me how to hold on to Mom with a belt while she walks with her walker.

The PT doctor came in and was glad she was eating better, and asked if she had any pain while he moved her legs, and she said, "No".

He said, "She seems to be doing better."

At 3:30 p.m., Mom was getting restless, and at 4:00 p.m. she received her medications. We ate dinner at 4:30 p.m., and then we headed to the library to look at the birds. She is somewhat fascinated by the birds, and it calms her to watch them. The small birds, finches and canaries mostly, are in a floor-to-ceiling aviary. It is a large cage, really. I'm beginning to feel like I am in a cage, but as I look at the patients around me, I can only imagine how they must feel. The tiny birds fly up and down in a cage--within a cage. The walls of the library around the aviary are filled with books of all kinds. I love to read, so I can visualize all the stories to be told in each one of those books. Yet, in each wheelchair around the room, also sits an intriguing life story to be told.

September 18, 2014

Ronnie's Notes:

I arrived at 7:35 a.m. Mom is up and dressed and is eating with the speech therapist. The therapist advised me that Mom was saying she was "really hungry" (probably because she did not eat her dinner last night), but then she kept putting her fork down, acting like she was full. When the front part of the plate is empty, she thought she was finished, so I turned the plate around and said, "You have a whole meal right there." The speech therapist told me that AD patients' vision is affected by their disease, and when they eat a portion of food off a small circle of their plate, they think they are done, so you need to move the food around on their plate so they can visualize the other food. She also said that studies have been done which show that AD patients can visualize their food and eat better off of a <u>red plate</u> set on a <u>white background</u> (table-cloth or place mat). Fortunately, I have some red plates for her at home, and we will try that.

In reviewing Mom's medication list printed off the nurse's computer, I just realized that her anxiety/depression daily mood stabilizer is not on there. The nurse said the doctor discontinued that medication two weeks ago, and that is just how long it takes for the medicine to leave her system. No wonder she's been so angry lately! When something is working, I don't understand why they would want to change it. I found the woman doctor and asked her why she took Mom off her mood stabilizer, and she said that when we talked previously, she questioned why Mom was on both the mood stabilizer and the sleeping pill because they were in the same group of medicines. (She believes because she posed this question to me, she was really telling me she was removing the medication.) I explained to her (again) that the one helps her to sleep, while the other one helps to stabilize her moods. She never told me that she was going to discontinue her mood stabilizer because I would have definitely told her that was not a good idea, since this medicine regimen was tried and considered to work very well for a number of years now. I also told her of studies that were conducted showing that the mood stabilizer may aid in halting the advancement of AD, so I would like her back on it. She agreed that she also heard of these studies, so she will restart the medicine today and noontime.

After a late lunch, I walked Mom up to the therapy room and spoke to the PT manager. She confirmed that Mom's balance score came up from 26/56 (last week) to 33/56. She told me that if the home evaluation next Thursday goes well, that also serves as the care conference, so Mom can go home three days or so after that—unless we request we want her to come home that weekend. Also, we decided that the PT, the OT, the nurse, and the home health aide will all be coming out of the nearby hospital, because that is where Mom was hospitalized for the hip replacement. We could set up PT on Mondays and Wednesdays and the OT on Thursdays and Thursdays, if we want someone to come every day.

I asked the PT manager if we can take off the restriction of pulling the wheelchair behind her when we are walking, and she said she would do that if we always know where the chairs are on the way, so we can get there if she needs to sit. She said that Mom walked pretty well without the walker except for turning or maneuvering in narrow spaces—so she is still high risk for falling. I walked with Mom back to her room. The OT was waiting for us to take her back to PT to recertify her, because mom met her goals for the first 30 days' stay. I don't think Mom did very well in this test. We came back to her room, and she wanted to lie down.

We went out to the courtyard, and I had her coat bundled up and we were sitting in the sun (it was about 68 degrees). We didn't stay out too long before she complained about being cold, so we went inside and got our suppers. She then got her nighttime meds, we dressed her in her pajamas and she was in bed at 6:45 p.m. I left at 7:15 p.m. Mom is nearing the end of her stay here. Every day I give thanks that no disaster has occurred.

I have seen very caring staff members in this nursing home. It is easy to distinguish the ones who truly care about the patients from the ones who don't. The therapists all seem to enjoy their jobs and perform with a smile on their faces. In my opinion, certified nursing assistants should receive better pay and continuing education for the level of duties and responsibility they bear.

September 22, 2014

Ronnie's Notes:

The PT had told us that it could take four to five days to order the wheelchair, which is then delivered within twenty-four hours before discharge. Everyone seems to give me a different answer regarding discharge. A nurse told me the patient has to have all the therapies the day before discharge, but has to stay until after midnight that night in order for Medicare to pay for it. They can have *no* therapies on the day of discharge. The therapists do not work on Sundays, so that is why I thought discharge would have to take place on a Tuesday. Talking to the PA today, she told me she did not know if that was true because the doctor discharges people on Mondays all the time. It's a wonder anyone can get discharged around here.

I spoke to the PT about Mom getting up and walking around in the mornings, and everyone down here just "thinks she's doing great", yet they do not do anything to prevent it, or supervise it. She is still a fall risk. She said they could put signs up in Mom's room. I asked her if the signs would be for Mom or for the staff? She said the signs would be for Mom to remind her not to get up (is she kidding me? Don't they know this by now?) I said Mom has not been able to read or comprehend the written word for about five years now. She would take no notice of any signs at all. She said then she would notate Mom's "care plan" so the staff understands the situation.

We watched television in her room at 2:00 p.m. She said she was tired, so the aide took her to the bathroom and got her in bed, but she didn't really fall asleep. She got her medications at 3:00 p.m. and wanted to stay in bed. I finally got her up at 4:00 p.m., and at 4:30 p.m. we ordered her supper. She is agitated this afternoon, very negative. Sundown syndrome continues to rear its ugly head in the afternoons. However, she ate a good dinner.

September 23, 2014

Ronnie's Notes:

I arrived at 7:55 a.m., and the RT was assisting mom with breakfast. She ate about half (she does not seem very hungry this morning). We watched television in her room for about an hour, and then the PT walked her down to the therapy room with her walker. In her PT exercise she did okay with balance when turning/bending, etc. I asked the PT about getting Mom a stationary bike for home and she suggested we get a "Restorator" from a medical supply store, or we can order one from their catalogs. A "Restorator" is the small pedal bike they have in PT that she can use with her hands or with her feet sitting in her chair at home. She also did some leg exercises with weights. After this, Mom walked without her walker back toward her room, but was soon breathing hard near the café and had to be wheeled the rest of the way. The therapist said she would do speech therapy after lunch because it is too noisy and crowded down in therapy right now. The RT came to get Mom for lunch at 11:40 a.m., and she walked down to the dining room. I have to leave now, but Jeanne will be here soon.

September 25, 2014

Ronnie's Notes:

I arrived at 7:55 a.m. I am told that Mom was sleepy today, and they got her up finally at 7:30 p.m. The nurses will try get Mom up from bed at 7:30 a.m. to acclimate her back to our time schedule, in order to prepare her to come home. The RT brought breakfast, but Mom appears to be rather "out-of-it" today. She doesn't like whatever he gives her. We came back to her room, and I helped her do some leg exercises to prepare her for walking at the home evaluation today scheduled at 11:00 a.m. I asked the nurse to give me Mom's noon meds crushed so we can take them home. I also informed her that I'll be gone Friday to Saturday, and I gave her Julie's schedule.

We had the home evaluation at 11:00 a.m. It went very well. They said everything is in place. I had taken up throw rugs and bought a couple industrial runners for the bathroom. The therapists tested the runners with the walker and said they do not catch—they will be fine (and safer than the slippery tile alone). Mom did some walking both with and without the walker in the house. They said they usually recommend a dining chair with arms on it, but they said she gets in and out of her chair without the arms just fine. I bought a raised toilet seat with handles and also a "Restorator" for arm and leg exercises. Her discharge is approved and is being scheduled.

The social worker now tells me that Medicare will not cover a wheelchair because PT classified Mom as "independent at home". I said I wouldn't consider her independent because we do everything for her and she cannot walk far without being winded. I said if we take her anywhere at all, we will need a wheelchair. She went back and spoke to PT, and they said she can walk too far on her own—Medicare won't cover a wheelchair. They recommended we get a "transfer chair" (is this the walker with 4 wheels with a seat that we have now?) I will have to look this up on the internet and maybe find a used wheelchair to privately pay.

We returned to the nursing home at 3:00 p.m., and she became hungry, so she ate an early supper. The nurse said that Mom's hip has healed much faster than some of the younger people she has seen (probably due to the surgeon's new anterior procedure, not having to cut muscle or tendon).

September 29, 2014

Julie's Notes:

I arrived at 8:30 a.m. Ruth is sitting in the open square down the hall from her room when I arrived, with a magazine in front of her but not looking at it. The nurse said she already had breakfast. I took Ruth in the wheelchair to the therapy room and was told she will have both PT and OT since they focus on those therapies the day prior to discharge. We worked on the jigsaw puzzle in the puzzle room for a short time. Ruth seems a bit irritated this morning, so we watched "Golden Girls," we did some exercises, and a chocolate protein shake was brought in. Ruth finished it all.

I found the RT at noon for lunch. Ruth ate a good lunch, had her noontime meds, and then went down to PT at 12:25 pm.

Ronnie's Notes:

I arrived at 12:25 p.m. I confirmed with the social worker that she ordered a transport chair, which is covered by Medicare (I learned that a transport chair is a portable wheelchair—I don't know why they didn't just describe it to me that way in the first place, rather than making such a big deal about a wheelchair not being covered). This is the type of chair I wanted for her anyway—it is more portable—easy to maneuver in and out of the car and around the house. It will be delivered in about a week.

The social worker gave the signed discharge papers to accounts receivable. I found Mom and Julie heading to PT. The head PT did the discharge testing. Mom was rated twelve out of twenty-four (anything less than nineteen is considered high risk for falling). She may improve somewhat with home PT, but being in the late stage of Alzheimer's will probably keep her risk level there. The head PT said that Mom has improved significantly since she first came in. She has worked really hard. She gave Mom a "graduation from rehabilitation certificate" and said the home evaluation went really well, so she is good to get discharged tomorrow. Yay! This is a milestone in reverse. Good news, for a change. So many people her age go into a nursing home with a hip replacement and never come out again. We are fortunate to have cleared this hurdle. It will be a glorious day when she walks out of here.

We came back to her room to rest at 1:50 p.m. The doctor came by and said she is ready to discharge tomorrow. They will cover her medications for one month, but pain meds are only covered for two weeks. Mom will need to see her family doctor within 30 days of discharge. I told him she has appointments to see both the family doctor and the surgeon this Wednesday. He asked if we had any questions—I said no, not really. It has been one very, very long month.

19

An excerpt from Mom's memory book regarding what her typical dates were like:

"I'll never forget my first date – but it wasn't really a date. I was staying with my sister Gladys in Ortonville. I had to spend all of my vacations there to help her with their four small girls. The neighbors next door took me to a dance in town with a friend of theirs. He was nice but about 10 years older. I was 16. My first real date was with a boy I knew from grade school. We met at a school dance and could dance well together. We usually went to the school dances. I was 17 years old. My sister and my dad were always looking for someone for me. Of course, their taste wasn't the same as mine. It never is.

I finally met Harold in October after graduating. We went to picture theaters and stopped for a hamburger & malt afterwards. He also introduced me to skating on roller skates, (dancing on skates). We both loved that. On Saturday nights we went dancing at the Ball Rooms, such as the "Grande". In summer, the big bands came to the outdoor dance pavilions, such as Glen Miller (our favorite). We loved that. It was very romantic. We usually always had a snack afterwards. We also did some horseback riding on Sunday afternoons. Most of the time, we paired up with another couple."

[Journal Entries]
October 9, 2014
Mom came home one week and two days ago. Every day has

been filled with the PT, OT, nurse, and home health aide. Now I sit on my porch (also known as my sanctuary), and as the sun goes down, it still reflects through the trees into the woods, giving the illusion of warmth on an otherwise chilly evening. It is somewhat like walking through a dark valley and looking up through the trees to see a sliver of light, as the sun tries to pierce the darkness. I like to take advantage of my sanctuary since the cold blowing snows of winter will be here knocking on our door, before too long.

I just got Mom settled in bed. The long, tedious days of the nursing home are behind us. Although it was a trial I would not want to repeat, God knew what He was doing in teaching me so much. No, it was not a perfect situation, as our daily log reflects, but I may have failed to record that I met many truly compassionate, dedicated people there and I am a better person for it. I also gained the benefit of the knowledge of these specialists. Several lessons come to mind: One is the studies showing that Alzheimer's patients actually eat better when their dishes are red and sit on a white background. Also, her shuffling gait, bending forward, and looking down at the floor when she walks are all symptoms of Alzheimer's, and not due to her chronic spinal problems. The medication trials/adjustments to relieve her sundown symptoms were helpful. I guess one could say I even got an attitude adjustment. I appreciate Mom even more now and I am more joyful. Mom seems happier, too.

A couple weeks ago, I read an article in the newspaper about Alzheimer's that caught my eye, as I like to stay informed. Apparently, researchers recently discovered that studies show that Alzheimer's patients tend to have a history of anxiety, depression, and sleeplessness. I find this interesting, but somewhat disturbing, if it is accurate. I don't recall Mom ever suffering from those conditions prior to being diagnosed with AD. However, my dad and I have suffered with bouts of these symptoms. I prefer not to think about what that could mean. I continue to exercise, take healthy supplements, and eat healthy foods, believing I will somehow avoid my mother's fate. I refuse to throw in the towel. My dad was mentally sharp. My doctor says my level of forgetfulness is normal for someone my age and with my level of stress. I choose to believe her.

October 20, 2014

The therapists, the nurse, and the home health aide that come to our home are all very helpful. I help Mom with her exercises on the days they are not here. We are utilizing the "Restorator", which I also call "the pedal bike", for Mom to exercise on at home. She is somewhat reluctant, but will acquiesce with just a little prompting. The goal is to make her stronger and less likely to stumble and fall when she gets up out of her chair, because she will not remember to take her walker on her own, and she gets up many times if I am out of sight in the kitchen or elsewhere in the house.

Jim and I still take Mom to breakfast on Sundays, but now when we go to the grocery store afterwards, we use their wheelchair cart. It is a wheelchair that she can sit in and I can push, but it has a basket on the front for our groceries. It is very helpful. Mom still loves to go out and ride in the car.

20

An excerpt from Mom's memory book:

(Giving an accounting of her brothers and sisters)

"Gladys was very quiet and didn't do any sports. She always had handiwork in her hands or a book. She had 4 daughters.

Clara (Sis) was more social and active. She was the one I was closest to. She divorced and married for a second time, but had no children.

Walter was always the choice one in our family. After my father died, he took care of my mother's finances. He married and had one son.

Fred was always in trouble, not bad trouble, but things were never dull. He married and had no children.

Arthur was the closest in age but we never did things together, except when he wanted to date one of my girlfriends in high school. [He was wounded during his service in World War II.] He had varicose veins in both legs. They should have been amputated but he wouldn't opt for it, so he had numerous operations. He was married. There were two daughters, but one died when she was 7 years old due to a doctor's incompetence."

[Journal Entries]

November 3, 2014

Can it be almost a whole month since I have written? The days are turning colder and the nights are colder still. No more warm breezes spent out in the sanctuary. Mom's PT ended last week, and we settled into our familiar daily routine with some

PT added to the mix. I had put off my "last resort" elbow surgery as long as possible, and now the pain and limited use has forced me to schedule surgery in less than two weeks; however, another ripple has come into our "back to normal" status. A chilling incident occurred which leads me to conclude that there is no "normal" where AD is concerned.

Yesterday, after breakfast, Mom made motions like she wanted to go to the bathroom, so I took her to the bathroom and waited there for her. After about five minutes, I saw there was no activity, so I asked if she wanted to walk around a little to see if that would help her to go. She did not respond. Her head dropped down to her chest and her arms hung limp. She was breathing shallow, would take some gulps of air, and then go back to barely breathing at all. The side of her mouth soon hung open to the side, and she began to drool. I yelled for Jim to call 911. As we waited for the EMS, several scenarios crossed my mind, but I believed she may have had a stroke. My adrenaline was pumping on overdrive. I thought we were losing her.

The EMS arrived and took her vitals, which revealed her heart rate and blood pressure to be extremely low. They laid her down on the floor, and she actually began to come around. It wasn't long before her eyes began to focus, and she smiled up at me. (Whew!) The EMS loaded her on the stretcher, and it was off to the hospital, once again, where we spent the remainder of that day. Blood tests, X-rays, CAT scans, EKG's, etc. etc. were done, and yet no cause was evident. They gave the episode the name of *vasovagal syncope*, which means something about a nerve that is pinched by sitting on the toilet, which then shuts off function to the brain. The cardiologist cleared the heart from having any involvement. The tests also revealed a urinary tract infection (UTI), elevated platelet counts, and slightly elevated kidney function. The cause of an elevated platelet count varies widely to be anything from the body having an infection, surgery, arthritis, IBS, or maybe an even more serious disease. However, she would be discharged from the hospital tomorrow with antibiotics for the UTI, and upon our visit to the primary doctor this week we will see if she wants to refer her to a hematologist.

I stayed at the hospital all day yesterday and today, now being mentally exhausted and adrenaline-sapped. I guess our new "normal" seems to include hospitals, medical tests, doctors and nurses' visits.

November 7, 2014

The long march through the "valley of the shadow" continues. The day Mom was to be discharged from the hospital, the doctor came into her room and advised that Mom's UTI proved to be extremely resistant to treatment, as well as extremely contagious. In fact, he likened it to be the UTI-equivalent of the "flesh-eating" bacteria that is so difficult to treat. The doctor believed Mom's passing-out episode could be attributed to her septic condition, which was due to the UTI. I was told that Mom would need to have a port installed, and would have to go back to the nursing home so they could administer the antibiotic drugs directly into her bloodstream. As we were waiting in her room for them to set up the nursing home stay, another doctor came in and said they found a very new-on-the-market oral drug that can treat the infection without needing to have a port installed. She would be able to come home after all.

November 13, 2014

It has been a week since Mom came home from the hospital and my primary duties have been washing and scrubbing everything repeatedly. Bleach has become my new best friend. The new medication proved to be successful in clearing up her UTI. Today we took Mom to the adult foster care home for respite care so that I could have elbow surgery tomorrow. The surgery will render me one-handed for several weeks, so Mom will be in respite for about three weeks. After numerous conversations with different anesthesiologists, I finally learned that they no longer use any of the anesthetics that affect the memory functions of the brain, so I don't have to be concerned about that for myself.

November 17, 2014

It sure is quiet around here. I have a fiberglass cast on my arm. Today the most peculiar thing occurred. Mom has a collection of beer steins, which she bought during her trips to Europe with my dad. The collection now sits atop the wardrobe in her room and hasn't been touched, other than dusting, since she moved in one and a half years ago. This morning, I was alone in the house. I had an eerie feeling when I came up from the basement and I heard the faint tinkling of a music box. Upon investigation, I found one of the steins has a music box, which mysteriously began to play "Auf Wiederschen". I believe that means "goodbye". There is no explanation as to why this music box would start playing on its own. Perhaps there are angels among us. Or, maybe my dad came for a visit?

21

An excerpt from Mom's memory book:

"I'll never forget when I was a youngster and at Christmas, we usually put the tree up on Christmas Eve. When I got older, my dad would make his own egg-nog for anyone that wanted to stop in. He would enlist my help in beating the egg yolks. It took quite a while. The children's Christmas program at church was held on Christmas Eve. I was usually in it. After, we were given a bag with an orange, apple, nuts & candy. We put up red & green crepe-paper streamers & bells for decoration. The tree was real, so it always smelled of pine. Of course, my mother baked many different cookies, also fruit cakes, stollen [a German Christmas cake] & even home-made candy. Christmas dinner was usually "goose". On Christmas Day, we went to my grandparents & different relatives' houses. When it was our turn, there were so many that the men ate first, then the children, last the women got to sit down to eat. As usual, the women cleaned up afterwards, while the men played cards. My mother always made new clothes for my doll. The first present I can remember was when I was 3 1/2 years. My father bought my mother a rocker & a small one for me. It is now Jeffie's."

[Journal Entries]
December 1, 2014
It is December already. I am not sure if "respite" means "my respite" or "mom's respite from me", but our three-week respite

is nearing an end. Mom will return home the day after tomorrow. The splint comes off my arm next week and our caregivers will help me in the meantime. We picked mom up from respite care and took her to Thanksgiving dinner at a fancy resort. Her gaze was hollow, and her steps were short and labored. As we began up the steps of the restaurant, her balance was shaky, and she began to reel backward, even with me holding her arm, but people rushed to our assistance and caught her before she fell. She seems to have gotten weaker during her stay in the respite care home. Respite care cannot provide the magnitude of physical therapy that we were able to provide for her at home, so we will step up her exercise again upon her return. Again, I tell myself, if she can gain in strength, this will reduce her risk of falling.

I have come to a heart-rending realization in our journey. Although I do not believe it is quite the time to call in hospice, I have actually begun to pray that God will take Mom home to Heaven peacefully, that He would end her suffering. This decision is not selfish; I prefer to have her with me. This road has led through a canyon fraught with briars, cliffs, and chasms that we have had to overcome, this is certain. Yet, even though she does not remember her role in my childhood, the vacations we took, the home she made for us, or even the man she was married to for fifty-nine years, when I look at her, *I* remember them. And that has been enough for me. But today I have turned a corner. The last four months, she has suffered. Just like a toddler who does not understand why they are in the hospital, why they hurt so much, why doctors come and go, I have sat at her bedside and watched her go through this. What does the future hold? While only God knows the timing for sure, we know this "valley" will continue to bring a steady decline leading to the end. I will pray for renewed strength and wisdom to see it through.

December 6, 2014

Mom returned home from respite care as scheduled and her walking abilities seem to have taken quite a step backward, as

I suspected. I can only assume she did not leave her chair too often while she was there. I suppose we cannot expect adult foster care homes to offer physical therapy as part of their service, but the level of decline was a surprise to us. I am beginning to suspect that the sedative currently prescribed may be contributing to her lack of energy and stamina, so today I will suggest stopping that medicine, because if she has no stamina to walk, I fear she may fall again. Her physical therapy program will be back in full swing now with the help of my caregivers and me. We'll see if this helps.

December 12, 2014

What a day. Another terrifying incident snuck up on us today. At two thirty this afternoon, I took Mom to the bathroom and brought her back and sat her in the rocking chair. I then headed into the kitchen to feed Nellie and crush Mom's meds. I peeked around the corner of the kitchen, and she was up and looking out the window. I turned back to finish my task when I was suddenly horrified to hear a heavy *"boom"* and *"thud"*. I immediately knew what had happened. Mom had fallen—again. I ran to her, and she was murmuring, "Help me, help me", as she lay face down on the living room carpet. My own heart was thump-thumping as my mind was churning, reliving the recent hip fracture, surgery, and extensive nursing-home confinement just a few months ago. This time it appeared she hit her arm and her hand on the coffee table, before crash-landing on her face. As evidence, her broken glasses were lying on the floor. She was able to move, and she sat herself up. Now I saw her nose was swelling and bleeding, and the middle finger on her left hand was bent sideways at the knuckle. It looked like her face took the force of the fall, broken only by her hand, as she reached out to catch herself.

A quick phone call to my next-door neighbor brought him over to help me get her up off the floor and into the chair. My hands were shaking trying to zip up her coat. I drove us to the ER where the obligatory CAT scans and X-rays were taken. Even though her nose had begun to turn black and blue, the only broken bone was the finger (thank goodness), nothing else. Her arm was pretty bruised. The finger was fitted with a splint and we came home. I fed her a late dinner, and then tucked her into bed. Once again, the circle of feelings has spun around to "guilt". Could I have prevented this? Even if I had been in the same room at the time, rather than around the corner, I doubt I could have prevented this. My thoughts are drifting more and more to hospice...

December 15, 2014

My physical therapist worked on restoring the use of my elbow and relieved some of the stress in my stiff neck today. She was telling me about caring for her brother in the end stages of his MS and how helpful hospice was for her. She said it may be helpful for me to call them. This afternoon when I returned home, our caregiver reported that mom's dentist now says that mom has a yeast infection in her mouth, and that this was likely caused by the mega-doses of antibiotics prescribed for her UTI a few weeks ago. The dentist prescribed a liquid medication that she is supposed to swish and spit five times a day. However, her AD befuddles these instructions, so she swallows it rather than spitting it out. No amount of verbal or visual instruction can break through her fog. I am weary. Today I called her doctor and got the referral to hospice. I called hospice and they will come out on Thursday to "enlist" her. It seems like an oxymoron that you must get "enlisted" for help to die.

December 23, 2014

I always believed I would know when the time was right to call in hospice, and indeed, the time has arrived. Since I called hospice, there has been a maelstrom of phone calls and visits from social workers, nurses, spiritual advisors, home health aides, and volunteer services. The hospice doctor will now be assuming her care, so I canceled the appointment she had with her primary doctor. Under hospice rules, any medical appointments with a doctor not affiliated with hospice will not be covered by Medicare. Also, if we have an emergency, we are to call hospice first, not 911, because if we call 911 directly, the ambulance will not be covered by Medicare, either, and we would have to pay the ambulance out-of-pocket.

My biggest fear about hospice is that they may force us to change or drop her medications, and also that she would no longer be able to leave the home. They tell me these fears are unfounded, that no significant changes will be made to her medications, and we are told we can take Mom out of the home as long as she is able to go. I am relieved. They are now my new support system and will be Mom's guardian angels here on earth, a god-send in this blackest time.

Sunday was our Christmas program at church. The last Christmas carol we sang was "Oh Come All Ye Faithful". As I stood arm-in-arm with Mom, she couldn't sing, but she indicated she recognized the tune by the nodding of her head. The tears began to accumulate in the corners of my eyes as my thoughts drifted to the probability that this would most likely be the last Christmas carol I would share with my mom in church. Nostalgic memories came floating back of Mom playing Christmas carols on our stereo in the early mornings of Decembers past, to wake us up for school. I did the same thing to get my boys up for school, (and they often tease me now about my "chipmunks" and John Denver selections). I have begun to play Christmas carols in the morning to help Mom to rise, because she has been refusing to get out of bed when I try to get her up. Christmas carols will always hold a special place for us.

22

An excerpt from Mom's memory book:

[giving an accounting of her father]

"I'll never forget my father. He was very strict. There were 3 boys and 3 girls in our family. I was the youngest. He was 6 feet, fair hair & skin, and slender. He had to leave school at 12 years old to go to work. Worked for [an automobile company] & designed the modern-day car radiator. [The automobile company] stole it from him so he quit & joined the police force. Had an appendix operation, developed varicose veins. We moved to South Lyon to a farm. He didn't like it & traveled by train to Port Huron to work every week. He learned the car radiator repair business. In 1926, he started his own business on Cheyenne in Detroit. The business was behind our house. He was a very hard-working person. Built the business up to very well-paying. Kept it until he retired & gave it to my two older brothers. He kept all his own records & tax reports. Both ankles had ulcers from the [varicose] veins, so he had to wear high shoes. He died at age 62, one day after his birthday. He had a heart attack."

[Journal Entries]

January 4, 2015

A new year has emerged from what you might call the "rubble" of last year. The holidays were very busy and culminated with us hosting our neighborhood euchre party on New Year's Eve. Jeanne sat upstairs while Mom was in bed, and the party was held downstairs in the finished basement. It was a risky venture, to be sure, but I am thrilled to report that there were no issues during the party, and in fact, there has been no emergency with Mom for a few weeks now. She is more unsteady on her feet each day. We keep her gait belt fastened around her waist at all times, and her walker is constantly in front of her.

Today I told her that one day we would both be in heaven and would have conversations about all the trips we took, and the houses we lived in and the little dog we used to have, Terry; then Mom looked up at me bright-eyed and nodding her head and agreed with me, just like she understood. It was as if a merciful window of memory was cracked open. She even looked up at me and said that I was going to make her cry. Her expression of feelings is so rare. It was all I could do to hug her and tell her that I loved her. I pretended that she really knew who I was, and who knows, for a fleeting moment, maybe she did. It was another moment of clarity that I will cherish.

January 5, 2015

A different nurse came today. I liked her very much. She took time to talk. She asked how Mom was eating, and I told her she was not eating much and I would often have to feed her. She said they go through a stage where they are always rooting around for food (I told her we were through this stage already). She said the next "stage" is not eating much, and then the organs become incapable of absorbing the nutrients until the body does not want the food, and will not accept the food. When this happens, even though I will try to feed her, she may vomit. I have never had someone explain this process to me before. It lessens the fear of the unknown, when you actually know what may happen. Yet, while being informed removes the fear of the unknown, I pray she will go quietly in her sleep before this disease completely ravages her body. We will fear no evil…

January 20, 2015

I could not take Mom to church yesterday. The weather turned bad, and her bowel problems seem to appear on Sundays, just around the time to go to church. Her afternoon anxiety has increased, despite the higher doses of the medicines that the doctor prescribed. Every day now I daydream about escaping this responsibility, and then the guilt settles in like a familiar overcoat. I do truly love her and treasure in my heart every facial expression and smile I can entice from her. This is the roller-coaster effect, up and down, stress and guilt. It is exhausting. Dinnertime is stressful. She continues to follow me into the kitchen, and doesn't listen to any direction.

January 31, 2015

Once again, we're on a theme-park ride, but this time it is a BM roller coaster, and the ride has come to a dead stop for a whole week. I'll have to talk to the nurse to get this ride moving again. They have ways to make that happen. I'm sure I will have to learn their ways, and do it myself.

At the time the social worker came for her first visit, she asked if we had funeral plans in place. We did not, but that got me to thinking and preparing. Today we met with the funeral home and made decision after decision. We even toured restaurants to arrange for the luncheon. It is a bittersweet relief to have these plans in place so the stress level may be toned down with one less fret lurking in the shadows. It was not an easy task, but the shoulder burden has eased a bit. Tomorrow I will send my sisters the results of our plans.

In a couple more weeks, Mom will go to the nursing home for respite care (arranged by hospice) for five days, while Jim and I go up north on a cottage-hunting expedition. It has always been my dream to have a lakefront cottage to gather with the kids and grandkids. Hospice offers this respite care and greatly encourages it. It is common to feel guilt for using respite care, and have fear of what could happen if I should leave her in the hands of others, yet hospice seems to understand this and encourages respite care. It is healthy for caregivers to separate themselves from the psychological stress and strain, and to rest from it, if even it's only for a short while. I hope the weather cooperates.

It will be Valentine's Day.

23

An excerpt from Mom's memory book:

[giving an accounting of her mother]

"I'll never forget my mother. She was short, 5'2", a little plump but not fat. She had to leave school at 12 years of age to help support the family. She was married at 17 years, had 6 children–Gladys, Clara, Walter, Fred, Art, and me, Ruth. She worked hard to raise her family. The house was always very clean and she was a very good cook. When my father died, she was 58 years old, but she would never take on responsibility for her finances or go out to have a good time unless one of us included her in our activities. She was independent in the places where she could walk—the closest store, the beauty parlor. When my brother moved her to an apartment when she was 80 years old, she made friends with 2 neighbors (single women), then she got quite social. They'd go out to eat, church, and shopping together. She died at 90 years of age, very suddenly."

[Journal Entries]

February 1, 2015

I have already made hotel reservations for our trip up north, and now the hospice social worker has called and said the nursing home refuses to take hospice patients right now because they have no beds available. She told me of another nursing home that is available; however, Jim and I previously toured that facility--I have memories of dirt and smells of urine, and I wouldn't take my dog there. Our trip had been scheduled for

February 12 through 17. What do I do now?

February 3, 2015

I have cancelled one night of our reservation at the hotel up north, and I lined up caregivers to spend the day and night, for an overnight stay. With having to make all new arrangements, respite turns out to be not much of a respite.

February 5, 2015

Lo and behold, the social worker has called once again, and now says that the original nursing home (where Mom stayed before) has agreed to take her on the twelfth, and there will be no more problems with them. She guarantees it.

February 10, 2015

I went to Bible study tonight and had a great conversation with another lady who agreed to pray for me that all would go well, and I would enjoy a true respite.

February 11, 2015

As I finish packing for Mom's stay at the nursing home, I experience a sense of apprehension that I will actually be leaving her in strangers' hands with absolutely no contact from me for five days. This will be a first time in so long that I can't remember how long. She is in hospice care now, and they will care for her there, but she is really in God's hands after all. This respite is a gift, and since God is giving me this gift, He will take care of every detail. This leaves me with the peace that passes all understanding.

February 12, 2015

I spent a couple hours today at the nursing home trying to get Mom settled into the exact same room she was in for rehabilitation after she broke her hip. I had to order and fetch her lunch from the dining room and help her eat it. The same nurse who was there the very first time I brought Mom there back in August was on duty. She took me aside and spent quite some time pulling Mom's medications up on her computer so she could reconcile them with me. As I was getting ready to leave, the nurse says to me, "You know we still don't have one-on-one care and we do not have the staff to feed her". Déjà vu. Here we go again. I can't figure out if she says this for her own protection, or if she really has Mom's best interests in mind. I know the hospice nurses will be there.

I like to give the benefit of the doubt, but now a mysterious peace came over me, and I just told her, "I won't be here for five days because I am going out of town and I'm leaving her in your capable hands". Then I left. This time, let's hope they do their jobs.

February 20, 2015

We enjoyed our respite, and put an offer on a lake-front cottage. It has a bedroom on the first floor, so we are looking forward to taking Mom with us this summer. I can picture her sitting on the deck, enjoying the lake view and activities of her great-grandkids. While we were gone, I resisted the urge to call the nursing home. I trusted that God would take care of her, and He certainly did, there were no falls or incidents. Since she came home, though, she is weaker and does not walk as well as she did before. The nurse at the nursing home told me they would not walk with her at all because they did not have an order from physical therapy, so she was pretty much kept in the wheelchair when she wasn't in bed. Bureaucracy—frustrating—but understandable, I suppose. Bureaucracy seems to overrule common sense these days.

24

An excerpt from Mom's memory book:

"I'll never forget when our family would go to our cottage on Grosse Isle. Usually, we'd go on Friday night & home on Sunday. Of course, the grass had to be cut all the time. When the weather was bad, we would burn coal in the pot-bellied stove and play cards. My brothers would go off with friends. Being the youngest I didn't have any place to go so would read lying in the hammock. Often, I'd take the oars for our small boat & walk up to the canal about 3/4 mile, then I would row myself around the different canals. When my aunts & cousins came on Sundays, I usually ended up babysitting them.

On special holidays when there were races or ball games, the men would all sit around the table-top radio & listen to them.

Sewing was an enjoyable pastime since I was about 5 years old. I had a suitcase with scraps of material from my mother's sewing. I used a 'cupie' [Kewpie] doll. My girlfriends & I would sit together sewing many hours.

There was no swimming or beaches. Any beaches were at private homes. My dad taught me to drive going to the cottage on Friday evenings & home on Sunday nights. As it was a stick shift, we chugged a lot, but he was patient."

[Journal Entries]

March 10, 2015

It is hard to write with little good to say. I used to exercise every day, but that fell by the wayside when I spent twelve-hour days at the nursing home in September. I find it difficult to focus, and my mind drifts to unknown places. I cannot retain a simple thought, or remember a thought I had just a minute before. I am really getting concerned about my lack of recall, but my doctor assures me that these symptoms are due to stress. I have seen people who are grieving that suffer the same sort of shut down. The only difference is, rather than a sudden loss, my grieving began fourteen years ago, as I've witnessed Mom's mind drift slowly away from us like a lone iceberg being pulled into the far reaches of a vast ocean to the horizon, until you can no longer see it. This grieving is further aggravated by the constant tension from the level of care she deserves to receive from us. Stress not only takes a toll on the mind; it takes a toll on the body.

I have had seven joint surgeries (shoulders, hips, and elbows) in the last seven years and what hair I have left is rapidly turning gray. No one, no matter how strong they are, can fight this disease on an island. You will not win, and your loved one will suffer even more. Just as it "takes a village to raise a child", so it also takes a village to carry the elderly to the end of their days on earth. I thank God for all the people He's placed in strategic times and places in my life to help us along this journey. With Him, all things are possible. Man is only made to see one piece of the jigsaw puzzle, but God sees the whole finished picture. An unknown author wrote, "When God pushes you to the edge, trust Him fully, because only two things can happen; either He will catch you when you fall, or He will teach you how to fly". It doesn't feel like my feet have been touching the ground lately. He's teaching me how to fly, and He's even caught me a few times along the way.

March 15, 2015

It has been a painfully long and bitter cold winter with a fair amount of snow, but this week we saw a break in the weather at long last. It still may take some time for me to shake the clutches of this cabin fever. One week ago, we were assigned to a different hospice nurse and doctor. This doctor claims that Mom's memory medication is not on their "formulary" of allowed drugs because it is probably not improving her memory at this time. Here we go again. I had to once again "reinvent the wheel" and prove to this doctor (as I had to prove to the last one) why taking her off the memory medication will cause her extreme agitation, as it did when I tried cutting it back a year ago. Don't even the hospice doctors talk to each other about their patients?

I researched the subject and gave the nurse printed pages in support of the "discontinuance syndrome" theory showing what happens to some people when this medicine is discontinued. The nurse gave my information to the doctor, and he said he is "willing to talk to me about it". I don't understand why a doctor would want to upset the apple cart. When a medicine regime is working, you don't change anything unless it may endanger her health. The nurse said that keeping Mom on the memory medication would not endanger her health. It would certainly not be conducive to "making her comfortable" in her last days to take her off this medication, and, therefore, would go against the standards set by hospice themselves.

I have the highest respect for the medical profession, but sometimes it seems today that each person has too many doctors, or "specialists", and those doctors are just not communicating with each other. I believe that better communication between the doctors themselves and between the doctors and caregivers would go a long way to preventing disasters from occurring. Perhaps a new course in medical school entitled "Intercommunication 101" would be helpful. Again, "bureaucracy," also known as "privacy laws," undermine common sense.

It is fortunate for me that Mom had one 90-day refill of her memory medication remaining from her regular pharmacy, and I filled this to bide us time until the doctor decides to "talk to me about it".

March 18, 2015

The nurse came for a visit today and told me that the doctor reviewed my research and has agreed to continue the memory medication.

March 20, 2015

The social worker, the chaplain, her caregivers, and the nurse, are all very upbeat. They all say Mom is doing so well. Who are they trying to kid? Is this some kind of conspiracy to try to make me feel better? No, I just don't have a Julie Andrews--type of optimism right now, since all I can see is the steady decline. I have sunk into an hour-by-hour, seven-day-a-week ritual of giving Mom the care that she needs, keeping up with the cooking, cleaning, and laundry, as well as grappling with my own health and medical bills. I pray to God for strength every day. How could anyone try to do this without Him?

Although the world seems very limited to me within these four walls at this point, it is important not to give up on our dreams. Your dreams can be a much-needed distraction and can actually keep you grounded in the knowledge that caregiving is not your whole life; it is only one season of your life. Do not allow it to define who you are, instead, allow it to confirm that you are accomplishing a very worthwhile function. And while it may seem thankless now, I like to believe that some day when I catch up with Mom in heaven, then she will know; then we will embrace as mother and daughter once again while she whispers in my ear, "Well done, and thank you".

25

An excerpt from Mom's memory book:

"When I was 10 years old, I'll never forget our grocery store. It was very small. There were no frozen foods. A few canned goods, but not like today. There was a small family-owned grocery store around the corner from us. It didn't have as much as the larger stores "A & P" or "Kroger". Actually, they were just starting up and weren't very large themselves. All the meats and sausages were fresh. There was also an "Awrey's" store near us. Oh! How we liked their jelly doughnuts. As to prices, it is hard to remember, but they were <u>very</u> low. Being raised during the Depression, so many people were out of work, they couldn't afford much. Milk was delivered by a milk-man. In the winter, cream would push up the top [of the bottle] for 2 or 3 inches. There were no refrigerators, so we also had ice delivered by a wagon. In the summer, the man would chip pieces off for us kids as we followed him down the street. We also had a "Sheeny". He went down the alleys to pick up reusable junk. We kids saved string and aluminum foil all week. We put it in a ball and he gave us a few pennies. There was a small candy store on the way back to school after lunch, where we could buy candy for 1 cent. What a treat.

[Journal Entries]

April 18, 2015

We are riding on the "Titanic". I know the iceberg is up ahead, yet there is no option to change course; this ship is doomed.

The caregivers and nurses say, "Prop up her feet so they don't swell" and, "Keep exercising her legs to keep her muscles moving". Unfortunately, her muscles are not affecting her movements; it is her mind that controls her movements, and her mind is not working properly. I continue to do what they say, but it seems to me that to keep trying their remedies, is like trying to bail out the Titanic with a beach pail.

Her decline in the last six months has been dramatic. Eating and walking are taking three times longer these days, and we have to take the wheelchair now wherever we go as a matter of course. Getting her in and out of the car is quite a challenge each and every time. This afternoon she was mumbling mostly unintelligible words, as is usual now, and I could pick up only certain words. However, I did hear her say that, "My sisters are over there waiting for me". I could not understand the rest. So tonight, as I was getting her ready for bed, I hugged her and said, "I love you mama", and as I held her, she held on to me for quite a while. Then I looked her directly in the eyes and said, "If your sisters and your mom and dad want you to go with them, it is okay for you to go, because I don't like to see you suffer here. I will probably see you in a little while, so it's okay for you to go". She didn't make any response, but I may have spied a look of relief on her face.

26

An excerpt from Mom's memory book:

"I'll never forget that my grade school was just 2 blocks from home. There was a crossing guard because we had to cross busy Grand River Ave. My first day of kindergarten was unforgettable. After school, my brother Arthur was supposed to pick me up. He didn't because he went off to play. I was crying so hard because I didn't know where I was. I fell into a ditch onto some glass and cut the palm of my hand. The principal found me & called my father. He took me to the doctor who probed for glass and stitched my hand.

Eventually, I made friends and was pretty good at my classes. There was an ice-skating rink on the school grounds. I loved it. It was during the Depression, so my parents couldn't afford skates. I wore my brothers' skates that they had outgrown. The toe was cut open on one skate, but I didn't care. When I was about 13, they bought me a pair of white figure skates. I was in Heaven.

Most of my teachers were very nice. I think I got a very good educational start from them."

[Journal Entries]

May 2, 2015

It was a beautiful Saturday afternoon today, so we took Mom to sit outside. Several neighbors came over to sit with us. We had an umbrella over mom's chair. She fell asleep in her chair, so I let her sleep a little while. Pretty soon I noticed her mouth was drooping and a little drool was dripping out. I went over to wake her up and she would not wake up. Her breathing was a little irregular, so we laid her down on the lawn (remembering what the EMS did the last time she passed out). Her face felt cool and clammy to the touch. I called hospice, who told me they would have a nurse call me, but they would not call 911 since she had a "Do Not Resuscitate" order. The nurse called me twenty minutes later and told us to get Mom into bed and elevate her head and she was on her way over.

The neighbors helped us to get her back into the wheelchair and then carried the wheelchair into the house. By this time, she had opened her eyes and began to come around. By the time the nurse arrived, Mom was more aware and responded to the nurse, so the nurse wrote in her report that Mom was "alert". Her blood pressure was 110/54, and her pulse was 43. This is low for Mom because her normal blood pressure is what is considered high for everyone else. My own heart beat eventually came back down to normal.

May 4, 2015

Mom can no longer stand on her own—another milestone. I spoke to the nurse today, and she ordered a new wheelchair (an actual wheelchair, not a transport chair). This fancy chair reclines and supports her head. Another nurse that I never met before came out to see Mom today. She was a nun. She was very helpful, loving, and joyful. She had the loving personality that I would like to have someday. I told her that Mom has been sleeping a lot, so she ordered some oxygen, believing that maybe the extensive sleeping is due to Mom not getting enough oxygen to the brain. Jim has to lift her into bed at night, and the aide comes in the morning to lift her into her wheelchair and dress her, etc. Daytime urination has ceased, so the nurse had to install a catheter, and I had to learn how to care for this device.

May 5, 2015

Someone created a wonderful contraption called the Hoyer

lift. It has a sling that I position under Mom and then the lift is lowered over her, like a crane. I then attach the straps to the lift, and Mom is lifted off her bed; the lift swings her around and places her into her wheelchair. I reverse the order at night to get her back into bed. This is a god-send because I can manage to do this all by myself.

May 7, 2015

Mom slept all day today and would only eat very little. Jeff and Wendi came to see her tonight, and she would not open her eyes. It appeared to them and to me that she may not make it through the night.

May 10, 2015

This week has been fraught with changes, changes and more changes. Old routines no longer apply. Friday, Saturday, and today (Sunday), Mom has been smiling, engaging, and even responding appropriately when asked questions. It is almost as if the fog of the Alzheimer's has been lifted, or maybe her spirit is compensating for what her brain can't do. Unfortunately, she still cannot walk, and is becoming so stiff, she almost slides out of her wheelchair. The stiffness renders her extremely difficult to dress and turn in bed. Her stiff feet are pointed (there is an actual name for this that escapes me at the moment). She has developed an ugly sore on her right heel. I get up in the middle of the night to turn her, so she doesn't develop bed sores. We keep a pad underneath her to aid with the turning process, but it is very difficult for one person. Our hired caregivers are not able to help with this at all, so the bulk of moving Mom is my responsibility. The hospice aide is an absolute angel and helps me when she is here. Jim also helps when he is here.

May 15, 2015

Despite the rigors of our current situation, we had someone stay with Mom today so Jim and I could make a one-day trek up North and back to finalize the purchase of our cottage. My life-long dream has finally come true with this lakefront cottage. We will be able to make good memories with children and grandchildren. In fact, we have named the cottage "Makin' Memories" in mom's honor.

Mom's care has stepped up many notches, and I feel the tension in every fiber of my being. Furnishing the cottage with projects and garage-sale finds has been a welcomed distraction the last couple of months. I have also found a wonderful respite care adult foster care home, and Mom will go there for two weeks beginning on May 19, so we can move in the furniture and make preparations for Mom to accompany us on our subsequent visits. The owner is so caring of all her people, and she spends a lot of time with them, talking to them and making them smile. That is really what matters the most at the end of life, just as it is at the beginning of life: loving people, nurturing people, and making them happy. Of all the facilities where Mom has resided, the adult foster care homes are the best. They are the most personal and have a home-like atmosphere where each person is loved and cared for like part of a family.

May 19, 2015

We celebrated Mom's ninety-third birthday this week. Hospice arranged the county transportation bus to pick us up today because they are wheelchair-accessible. Three neighbors carried Mom in her wheelchair out of the house and down the porch steps. Mom did not like the bus ride and became very anxious. I spent the next three hours at the home filling out paperwork before the bus came back to pick me up since I had no ride home. But this time, the ride home took an hour and a half due to the long route, and the many stops we had to make along the way. This day, it just so happens that our street was being repaved, so the bus had to drop me off at the end of my road, and I had to walk the rest of the way home. Just another day in the life of a caregiver. The unusual has become the usual.

27

An excerpt from Mom's memory book:
(Giving an accounting of her grandparents):

"My grandparents from my mother's side and my father's side came from Germany around 1875. A few of my aunts and uncles were born in Germany. I did have a family tree, but am unable to find it. My mother and dad were born in Detroit. I know that my grandfather on my dad's side was a builder in Germany. He built their nice house here but then he worked for [an automotive company] & got his 50-year watch from them. My mother's father worked at the Woodmere Cemetery. He was in college in Wittenberg, Germany to become a Pastor, but they immigrated here before he finished his schooling. All my grandparents spoke German and knew very little English. My mother & father both went to German Lutheran schools. They had to leave when they were 12-years-old to go to work. Their families were large & they needed the money. They would never teach us German so we couldn't converse with our grandparents very well. My father's parents lived until their late 80's. My mother's parents lived to their 90's. My mother's, mother's family had a large farm in Germany. She had 2 or 3 sisters. When she came to America, her family gave her a portion of the farm for her passage.

I have seen many dramatic changes in my lifetime. Air travel didn't start until after World War II. Of course, a lot of household appliances are here. The refrigerator was just an ice box where had to buy a block of ice for it. When I was very young, my mother cooked on a wood-burning stove. It did come in handy in the winter when we would race downstairs to dress in front of it because there wasn't much heat in the house. Crime has escalated. We could leave the house unlocked. Our cars were always left unlocked with the windows open. No one broke in. There was no such thing as men & women living together or having babies out of wedlock openly. When we dated, I believe we had more things to do such as movies, roller-skating rinks, dancing in ballrooms. These things are around today, but I guess they aren't sophisticated enough for the young ones. There was no such thing as computers or outer space travel. I think I liked our way better. It was more relaxing and less complicated.

I would like my epitaph to read that I've always tried to be honest and helpful and have loved my husband, the three girls & their families."

[Journal Entries]

June 4, 2015

What a wonderful time Jim and I had at the cottage, boating, golfing—even the work of cleaning and setting up the cottage was a fun kind of work. Such a peace came over me just brushing the water seal on our front porch. For two whole weeks, I tried not to worry about Mom. I knew she was in excellent hands with the staff there, as well as hospice coming to visit. They had my phone number if there was an emergency, and I was only a couple hours away. Jeff drove me to the AFC home to pick up mom yesterday, and then Mom and I had to wait about two hours for the bus to bring us home. This time the ride was much more pleasant. After they fastened the multiple straps to secure her wheelchair, I sat directly across the aisle from her, where she could see me this time, so she would be less anxious.

I scooched over to the edge of my seat and reached for her hand. As we held hands, she lightly stroked her thumb over the back of my hand, and I closed my eyes. We didn't have to speak, she was calm and I was calm, totally different from the first ride.

As we clutched each other's hands this way, I was transported back to a world I knew long ago, where she was the mother and I was the little girl. Neither one of us was willing to let go of that moment, so we stayed that way all the way home. Her peace showed in her smile. She was not anxious at all this time. It is healing to let my mind wander to those kinder memories, and I am thankful for each moment we have together. I often tell her how much I love her. Sometimes, in a soft voice, she'll whisper, "I love you, too", those words that bubble up from her spirit, a spirit that is untouched by disease. I am more convinced than ever that her spirit controls those words, her brain does not. Disease cannot kill the spirit. Thank God.

June 12, 2015

Mealtimes have become an hour-long labor of patience. Even chocolate desserts do not taste good to her anymore. Yesterday the nurse collaborated with the doctor, and due to Mom now having open bed sores, her pain medication was switched to morphine. She has been quite talkative today. Maybe the change is for the better. It breaks my heart to see these unavoidable bed sores, and we treat them several times a day, as directed by the nurse. The nurse says they result from a nutritional lack due to less food intake. This is all a result of the AD running its course.

June 14, 2015

Jim and I went out for a couple hours yesterday, leaving Mom with the caregiver, and when we arrived home, Mom was hunched over in her wheelchair. I put her to bed, and I believed she was just tired since she already had dinner and her nighttime medications. Today, however, she is extremely lethargic. She ate half of a waffle for breakfast, a small amount of her sandwich for lunch, and could not eat her dinner. She also would not drink much. Her posture was rigid and slumped in her wheelchair, seeming to be semi-conscious most of the day. I called the nurse who said to cut her morphine back to every other dose. In actuality, the last dose I administered was at 10:30 a.m. If, indeed, the morphine is causing her non-responsiveness, then we should know by tomorrow. All other medications are stopped.

June 17, 2015

It has been a two-day span that feels like an eternity. Monday morning, Mom continued to be sleeping, mostly non-responsive. However, I witnessed her reaching her hand up to the ceiling and looking at the ceiling like there was something (or someone) up there. She even began to make hand gestures to whoever she saw there and opening her mouth like she wanted to speak.

When the aide came, she had a difficult time washing her because she was so rigid and stiff. The nurse came out, and what she told me was hard for me to process. It is the beginning of the end. Mom continues to refuse food and drink, although her vital signs on Monday were still good. All meds have been stopped except the morphine and her nitroglycerin patch. Of course, I had fear that her anxiety would be way out of control after stopping the medications, but that did not happen. Although on Monday the nurse pronounced Mom's lungs were clear, today the nurse is hearing rattles, which means some fluid is building up in the lungs. The nurse says the end could come at any time. Life cannot be sustained long without food and drink. She said Mom could pass within a week, but probably not more than ten days, although it could also occur quickly. Everyone is different, and it is very difficult to predict. Although I tried to prepare for this, and we certainly had enough time to do this, it does not make it easier or less sad. The loss has already seeped its way into the recesses of my soul. Today, as she grabbed my hand, I thanked her for sewing all my dresses when I was young, and for knitting all those sweaters, afghans, and baby clothes, and for cleaning my scraped-up knees and for always being there when I needed her, and how very much I appreciate her.

June 20, 2015

Laurie has been here the last four days. We have sung songs to Mom and regaled her with our childhood memories, ever believing that she could hear us and understand. Yesterday, when the nurse was here, she said Mom had a five-second sleep apnea (with no breathing during that time), although all her other vital signs were stable. This afternoon, the apnea increased to fifteen to seventeen seconds. Tonight, I counted one at twenty-four seconds, then she takes six breaths, and then long apnea again. I called the nurse tonight who told me the end could come within a few hours.

The aide says the spirit overrules the body and they can hang on when they are waiting to see someone. Is there someone she could be waiting to see? Mom may be waiting until Leslie arrives from Atlanta before finally letting go. There are few words to describe how emotionally bone-weary I am in the darkest part of my "valley". I check on her periodically throughout the night. This is the time when you hope you have said all you need to say to your loved one.

June 21, 2015

Leslie and her family arrived from Atlanta. Mom was not as talkative today, but her eyes focused on Leslie, so she knew they were here. Her breathing is more even today, but there is a gurgling sound with each breath. She had refused food and water for a week now. I don't know how much longer this can go on.

June 22, 2015

The aide came to give Mom a bed bath today and because of Mom's active resistance when she tried to turn her, she believes Mom will still be with us two days from now for her next visit. The nurse came and said Mom's blood pressure has dropped to 98/46, and her pulse has gone up to 90 BPM. She said this is one of the end signs. She predicts Mom could leave us within twenty-four hours. I could tell all afternoon and into this evening that Mom's breathing is becoming shallower.

June 23, 2015

At midnight, I rose to administer Mom's scheduled dose of morphine. Her breathing was very shallow—sleeping peaceful. I kissed her brow and said, "You are my sunshine. I love you and will see you tomorrow sweet mama". At 1:30 a.m., Jim checked on her, and she was still breathing restfully. At 2:30 a.m., I woke up suddenly. I went to her room, and I saw that she had left us. She took her last breath in this world and her next breath in a much brighter one. She slipped away quietly into the night.

In days of old, when someone would die, it would be said that they, "gave up the spirit", but the way I see it, when a body becomes diseased and the biological functions shut down, it is more like the spirit, "gives up the body". She gave up her body. The body is just a biological vehicle for the spirit to travel in during its stay here on earth. Her worn-out body could no longer hold her vibrant spirit that yearned to be normal and free from disease. I will miss you, Mama. I went to Leslie's room, and she said she also woke up suddenly at 2:30 a.m. Hospice was called, and the nurse arrived at 4:00 a.m. to make the pronouncement. Hospice then called the funeral home, and they came to carry her away from us at 6:00 a.m. The rest of this day consisted of making phone calls and confirming funeral arrangements and working out all the myriad of details. I am glad Leslie was with me. When Leslie phoned her daughter Leta, she said she also woke up unexpectedly at 2:30 a.m. I like to think that Mom was making her rounds to say good-bye.

We all knew this day would come, but it does not seem real, being too caught up in the busyness, with no time to reflect. Now, as I look back, it occurs to me that as the time marched on and the disease progressed, she became more and more dependent on me. Just as her mind became more child-like, her needs became more demanding, like a child's, so now the void that is left is great. My life revolved around caring for her. The saving grace is my knowing that now she is whole and there is no more confusion, only clarity, joy, and love as she dwells with her loved ones who have gone on before. What a wonderful reunion she must have had with her parents and sisters and brothers that she spoke of so recently, as well as with my dad, as Jesus finally took her "home", where she always said she wanted to go, for so long.

So many people have expressed their amazement that I would take my mom in to live with me and care for her. I tell them that sure, sacrifices have to be made, and those sacrifices only increase as time goes by. I had no idea what was in store for us, but it was worth the sacrifice. What could possibly be more rewarding or important than taking care of your loved one and easing their final days on this earth? It was so worth it. When people try to protect their heart from the pain of losing a loved one, or for whatever reason, they may stow them away in a nursing home, but they are robbing themselves of so much more than they could have imagined. In our area, most nursing homes have an impersonal clinical atmosphere, and the care can be stilted by bureaucracy and overworked staff. The individual's emotional needs are overlooked, and many times, the physical needs, as well. I understand this may be the only option for some people. But if given the opportunity, why not care for them? What a privilege it has been. My journey wasn't perfect, and I made mistakes, but I know I did the best I could do, and I shudder to think what would have happened to her if we weren't there for her.

PART 3

A MESSAGE FROM HEAVEN

1

[Journal Entries]

July 23, 2015

She left us one month ago today. She was plucked from this "valley" and taken to the pinnacle of the mountain, but I am still left in our "valley". The fog is starting to lift around my ankles. Just because your loved one isn't physically here anymore, doesn't mean your world has stopped turning, even though sometimes it feels like it has. There is still much to do. Some people keep their loved one's room like a sort of shrine, as if they are hoping their loved one will come back to use it, unwilling to let them go. Other people clear the room out as soon as they can, possibly because it hurts too much every time they would look at the room, being reminded that their loved one will not be back to use it. There is no right way or a wrong way to grieve, but I suppose I am closer to the latter type. I was glad when Laurie came over and helped me to bag up Mom's clothes. I kept only a few select items—sweaters she had knit herself, a couple jackets and tops I had gifted to her for special occasions. It was difficult to look at the clothes that I dressed her in every day. My sisters took a few knick-knacks, and I kept some.

The day I dropped off some surplus supplies to her "senior center" adult day care facility, they gave me an art project she did during her stay there, along with an article with that had her photo in it from their newsletter. My self-control began to crumble, and I began to blubber before I could even reach the door. There are good and loving people in the world. I still try to avoid going into her room, but if I must go in to get something, I try to take care of at least one or two items, if I can, and this way, it will eventually be done.

August 7, 2015

I finally completed the last of the "Thank You" cards to all the people who gave flowers, donations, gifts, cards, or just visited the funeral home to be with us. I took extra time and effort to word these cards because it meant so much to me that these people took time out of their busy schedules to show they care for us and are hurting with us.

August 11, 2015

This morning the melancholy settled over me like a heavy blanket. I was missing Mom and recalling that in her more lucid years, she loved birds, just as her mother did before her. I have my grandmother's cement bird bath sitting in my back yard. This love of birds is evidenced by all the bird figurines of all shapes, styles, and compositions from her that now grace the nooks and crannies of my home. I was overcome by the loss of her today as I walked out onto my back deck "sanctuary" and eased down into my white wicker rocking chair. Just a few seconds later, I detected a loud "whirring" sound, which I believed was a bumble bee. As the whirring sound approached, I watched this tiny object fly into my sanctuary; it turned sideways, and to my delight, I discovered it was a hummingbird. The next thing I knew, it flew right up to me and actually hovered in front of my face, like we were having a non-verbal conversation. As we continued to stare in awe at each other, I marveled at its shiny metallic colors of red and green. I began to sense the warm arms of comfort and peace wrap themselves around me. A message from my mother, perhaps? Then, all at once when I blinked, the hummingbird circled around me and flew away. What a curious, but comforting joy that was for me.

September 9, 2015

It is still warm this week, but summer is waning and fall is inevitable. I've been keeping busy this summer going up to the lake, painting furniture, and entertaining the family and neighbors. However, keeping busy, although it seems to allay the grief, may just delay the grief, because when I come home, it is waiting for me there in the dark corners of Mom's room, in her never-ending estate-settling, and in her empty chair. Oh, what I would give to have her back with me, stealing cake again from the kitchen just one more time. There is also that ever-nagging question of, "Was there something more I could have done so that she could still be with us?" But then I sadly recall the final suffering she endured, and I could not wish that on anyone. Jim assured me that without our diligent care, she would have passed on years sooner than she did. So, I will try not to dwell too much on the end of life when there are new beginnings out there every day, like watching the grandchildren, or experiencing new discoveries. The seasons turn, and, "there is a time to be born and a time to die…"

2

No one knows what the future holds for them, or how they will leave this world and travel to the next. It would be ideal to go to sleep one night and just wake up in heaven, leaving this earthly body behind without all the pain and suffering that comes before. My fears of losing my memories has not been so much for what will happen to me, but rather the burden it would place on my husband, or eventually, my children. Jeff and Wendi have been like pillars of strength for me by offering their help to care for Mom over the last number of years.

One day, Jim and I were discussing Mom's care, as well as our possible futures, and Jeff told us that he and Wendi had a plan. With a sparkle in his eye, and a mischievous smile on his face, he said not to worry, it is their plan to buy property to build a compound. They will put several cottages on the property, one for each set of parents to live in, and then every day they will drive a golf cart around to hand out medications, and that is how they plan to take care of us all when we get older. We settled in to an easy laugh. We all know there is much more to caregiving than that, but there is an underlying thread of comfort woven through his words.

When you are walking through this journey, aging, and possibly your health isn't as good as it used to be; and you are facing death, whether it be your death, or a loved one's death, you experience a shift. The shift is in the line drawn between what's important and what's not. Love and family become all-important, while everything else tends to get caught in the brambles and is kicked by the wayside. Love becomes the peaceful, quiet waters we are led beside, and our family is the soft green pasture that cushions us as we lie restfully safe, secure, and unafraid, with our Divine Guard standing close by.

3

Grief is a natural and normal reaction to a loss. You need to go through grief to heal. I attended a bereavement group, and it gave me some very useful tools for healing. Grief can bring a wide range of emotions ranging from profound sadness to anger. It is important to remember you don't need to "be strong". Grief will not go away faster if you ignore it; there is no time limit to grieve, and it's okay to talk about the loss. Since I was aware that Mom's disease was terminal, I may have tried to prepare in advance, and I certainly began to grieve in advance; however, no matter how prepared you may feel, the actual death can still cause intense reactions. Grief can cause a wide myriad of reactions, including shock and disbelief, anger or resentment, guilt, fear or anxiety, deep sadness, physical problems, and yet eventually, hope and personal growth. There are many healthy ways to cope with grief and there is plenty of help whenever you need it.

Caregivers need to be aware of depression, and grief can also bring depression, but prolonged depression is a medical condition that can be treated. It is important after the loss of the loved one that you've been caring for so long, to now pay attention to the "self-care" that you may have been putting off: eat the proper foods, exercise regularly, get an adequate amount of sleep, and schedule those long-neglected doctor appointments to bring your own medical care back into focus.

Equally important, the "emotional self-care" must now be attended to: seek counseling or a group that will address your emotions, keep a journal, meditate or do relaxation exercises, maintain healthy and safe boundaries and make time for leisure or fun activities. I have resumed my exercising and my focus has improved. My recall is getting better. Look to your faith; God loves you and is there for you. Reach out to people you trust. Consider lighting a candle, visiting your loved one's resting place, planting a tree or bush in a place that was special to your loved one, and/or place the photograph in a place of prominence where you can see it often.

It is important to face your grief and deal with it. There is no shame in crying, it doesn't mean you are weak. Showing your true feelings to others may also help them to face their feelings. People grieve in different ways. Respect others and the way they grieve, because they will not all grieve the way you do.

4

I learned so much from the caregiver experience. For one, I learned that assisted living homes may be a good fit if needed in the early stages of Alzheimer's or dementia, but due to limited staff and the patient being isolated in their rooms with little or no supervision, these situations are not ideal for the patients in the later stages of the disease. There are also assisted living homes that are referred to a "Memory Care Facilities". Be prepared, because these can be quite costly. Additionally, I learned that nursing homes can be very perilous for Alzheimer's/dementia patients due to staff rotations and limited care per person. No one should just "drop" their loved one off at a nursing home and expect they will thrive there.

Today we are living in the midst of a global pandemic and it has been proven that the elderly in nursing homes are the most vulnerable. To add insult to injury, for many months, family members were not even allowed to visit! I can only imagine the horrors that went on behind closed doors without family caregivers being allowed to oversee the care, feeding and well-being of their loved ones. I do not believe my mother would have survived in the nursing home where she went for rehabilitation, without our caregivers and me giving her the constant supervision and intervention that she so desperately needed there. I believe nursing homes need vast changes in their systems to accommodate Alzheimer's/dementia patients who are there for a post-surgery rehabilitation. (I cannot speak for long-term care in nursing homes because my experience was not associated with that.)

If I was not able to care for my loved one in my home, my facility of choice would be a reputable Adult Foster Care (AFC) Home. These facilities have the smallest caregiver-to-patient ratio, and more individualized care. They are given their own bedrooms, but upon waking, come out into a "living room" or common area where they can associate with other patients. This situation is more home-like, and the people I have seen there are much less anxious and better cared for.

I understand there are many situations and reasons where people cannot become a caregiver and take their loved ones into their own homes. However, I think each person has to carefully examine their hearts for those reasons. Are they legitimate reasons, or could they be excuses? Being a caregiver is certainly challenging and I was fortunate to have help. Bringing my mother home to live with me was the best thing I ever did! I have no regrets. Our elderly loved ones still have so much to teach us. Even despite the fact that my mother did not recognize me as her daughter, we established a deeper relationship together than we ever had before. I was granted the opportunity to re-live good old memories, and forge lasting good new memories. I treasure this time I had with my mother.

What could possibly be more important than caring for your loved one in their final days? Certainly not money, status, busyness, or "freedom". With the current pandemic(s), skyrocketing costs of assisted living homes and outside care, and the population living longer than ever before, it makes more sense than ever to take your loved one in to live with you, and for some people, that is their only option. But be careful not to look at it as a burden. It is a blessing. It should be your first choice, if possible, not the "last resort". The disease can be managed and your loved one can still enjoy their life with you.

There are in-home caregivers for hire, visiting physicians, nurses, physical and other therapists, and many resources out there to help you on your caregiving journey. There are also organizations giving information, and government agencies for assistance. Don't hesitate to look to local churches (even if you don't currently attend one), because they are always looking for ways to serve. If you don't know the answers, seek out someone who does.

5

In the bereavement group I attended shortly after my mother passed, there were discussions between several attendees regarding unexplained experiences with birds. After the loss of a grandmother, the granddaughter saw a yellow bird on the window sill, yet when she left that room and went into another room, the bird was there on that window sill; and each room she went into that day, the bird was there, perched outside on the window sill, looking in at her. Another attendee shared that she saw bright red cardinals outside every window, a favorite bird of her loved one. And finally, when one attendee came into her bedroom, a butterfly was sitting on the pillow of their loved one's side of the bed. A profound peace enveloped her as she saw the butterfly rise up, fly away and disappear.

Science could not explain away such phenomena. Such happenings are too uncanny to be mere coincidences. These peoples' experiences seem to represent special supernatural connections to their loved ones, just like my hummingbird connected with me. The Bible essentially says that no one can fathom what God has prepared for those who love Him. Could these critters be winged heavenly messengers, dispatched by our loved ones, to lavish us with peace and comfort during our time of grieving? I like to think that they are. My blessings to you whatever journey you face now, or in your future.

Thank you for reading this book. It is my hope that you gleaned information that could help you. If so, please write a review of your reading experience on Amazon/Kindle and Goodreads, or other review sites. Thank you again!

ABOUT THE AUTHOR

R. R. Skrycki

R.R. Skrycki is a contributor to the books 'Across the Way", "Horse Tales for the Soul - Volume 7" and "Who's Who in American Poetry" as well as publishing numerous other short stories and poems. She was also the editor of "The Hartland Christian Soldier" newsletter. She wrote "Stolen Cake" to inspire other caregivers who may be struggling. She resides with her husband and dog, Mattie, in Michigan.

Made in the USA
Monee, IL
03 November 2020